I0633745

CALGARY PUBLIC LIBRARY

JUN   2018

SHEET PAN COOKING

GOOD
HOUSEKEEPING

SHEET PAN COOKING

70 EASY RECIPES

★ GOOD FOOD GUARANTEED ★

HEARST BOOKS

HEARSTBOOKS

An Imprint of Sterling Publishing
1166 Avenue of the Americas
New York, NY 10036

GOOD HOUSEKEEPING is a registered trademark of Hearst Communications, Inc.

© 2017 by Hearst Communications, Inc.

All rights reserved. No part of this publication may be reproduced, stored in a retrieval system,
or transmitted in any form or by any means (including electronic, mechanical, photocopying, recording, or otherwise)
without prior written permission from the publisher.

Every effort has been made to ensure that all the information in this book is accurate.
However, due to differing conditions, tools, and individual skills, the publisher cannot be responsible for
any injuries, losses, and/or other damages that may result from the use of the information in this book.

ISBN 978-1-61837-245-1

The Good Housekeeping Cookbook Seal guarantees that the recipes in this cookbook meet
the strict standards of the Good Housekeeping Research Institute. The Institute has been a source of
reliable information and a consumer advocate since 1900, and established its seal of approval in 1909.
Every recipe has been triple-tested for ease, reliability, and great taste.

Distributed in Canada by Sterling Publishing
c/o Canadian Manda Group, 664 Annette Street
Toronto, Ontario, Canada M6S 2C8
Distributed in Australia by NewSouth Books
45 Beach Street, Coogee, NSW, 2034, Australia

For information about custom editions, special sales, and premium and corporate purchases,
please contact Sterling Special Sales at 800-805-5489 or specialsales@sterlingpublishing.com.

Manufactured in China

2   4   6   8   10   9   7   5   3   1

www.sterlingpublishing.com
www.goodhousekeeping.com

GOOD HOUSEKEEPING

EDITOR IN CHIEF
Jane Francisco

FOOD DIRECTOR
Susan Westmoreland

CONTENTS

Rye-Crusted Pork Chops & Apple Slaw (page 65)

Foreword

Like most working people, I am always on the lookout for delicious ways to get weeknight dinner on the table—stat! And lucky for me, my days in the Good Housekeeping Test Kitchens give me the opportunity to help create new recipes for these meals every day.

I confess I'm in love with sheet pan cooking. It's the simplest, yummiest solution to dinner I know. Why? Without getting too technical, roasting meat, fish, and veggies at a high temperature concentrates their flavors and caramelizes their sugars and proteins, so in a short amount of time you'll get delicious results.

You've probably been roasting veggies for ages, and know that asparagus tastes, well, more asparagus-y, ditto for carrots, green beans, cauliflower, and just about any vegetable you've set in the oven. Okra was a revelation—sweet, a little crunchy, and not a trace of slime!

This same phenomenon happens with proteins, too. Never has a chicken breast had such flavor! Let *Sheet Pan Cooking* be your guide to making complete meals in the oven. (Yes, there are breakfast, brunch, and dessert options, too!)

The variety of flavors and textures that sheet pan cooking can produce might surprise you. In the chicken chapter alone we feature Crunchy Deviled Chicken, yummy, sticky Honey Mustard–Glazed Chicken Bake, and another of my favorites, Spanish Chicken & Peppers. Or maybe you're in the mood for the Spicy Drumsticks.

Craving meat? I'm a big fan of Rye-Crusted Pork Chops & Apple Slaw. Also the Feta & Mint Mini Meatloaves and the Cheeseburger Tostada are family favorites. Something Fishy? Try Honey-Soy Glazed Salmon, crispy Fish & Chips, or Roasted Shrimp & Poblano Pepper Salad. For Meatless Monday, whip up the Pizza Primavera, Falafel with Cucumber & Tomato Salad, or maybe the Sweet Potato Cakes with Kale & Bean Salad.

If you're in more of a breakfast frame of mind, check out the Smoky Tater Hash. Or if you want to wow the child (of 6 or 60) who has a thing for breakfast pastries, make the Glazed Berry Tarts. From Sparkly Apple Slab Pie to Sweet & Salty Zucchini Bread Cookies, the sheet pan desserts are sweet satisfaction.

So get out your sheet pan (or check out our pick for a new one), toss together a few ingredients, roast, and enjoy.

SUSAN WESTMORELAND
Food Director, *Good Housekeeping*

Introduction

When it comes to foolproof family dinners, nothing is more forgiving than roasting, baking, and broiling. These high-temperature techniques are hassle-free and hands-off. Most important, these methods develop great flavor and can be done on one versatile piece of equipment, a sheet pan.

Good Housekeeping Sheet Pan Cooking provides everything you need to put a fresh, homemade dinner on the table in a snap. And the best part? After enjoying a delicious meal there is minimal clean up.

The Only Pan You Need

A good sheet pan is hard to find. But we've got one—well, 30. We keep that many 18 x 12-inch jelly-roll pans in the test kitchen. They're perfect for roasting and with 1-inch-high sides, they allow for great browning but still catch pan juices. We prefer aluminum-coated steel or aluminum to nonstick pans. The surface of aluminum sheet pans ensures that vegetables, meats, and sweets brown beautifully. It also doesn't scratch easily, which means it lasts longer. When testing these sheet pan cooking recipes, we've learned that dark-colored pans hold too much heat and overbrown foods. So go light—even if you chose a baking sheet with a nonstick finish. Given their versatility and longevity, sheet pans are a bargain, usually at under $20 apiece. Sometimes labeled "half-sheet pans," they're available at many home supplies stores or online.

Sheet Pan vs. Jelly-Roll Pan

A sheet pan is a metal sheet with one or two sides bent up for easier handling. Its design allows air to circulate freely around the food so it bakes and browns evenly. A jelly-roll pan (either 15½ x 10½ inches or 18 x 12 inches a.k.a. a half-sheet pan) has 1-inch-high sides and is perfect for making cake rolls (see pages 118–119); it can stand in for a sheet pan in a pinch. It is also a terrific roasting pan for veggies and more. For these recipes, either a sheet pan or jelly-roll pan will be effective.

Vegetable Roasting 101

You can roast just about anything, but vegetables especially benefit from the high, dry heat of the oven. Their flavor becomes concentrated and their natural sugars caramelize, transforming them into richly satisfying sides.

Refer to this helpful chart for cutting instructions, cooking times, and seasoning suggestions for perfect oven-roasted veggies every time. For every 2 pounds of vegetables, toss with 1 tablespoon of olive oil prior to roasting. Spread the vegetables on a sheet pan in a single layer, with space between the vegetables to allow heat to circulate around them. If the vegetables are overcrowded, they will steam rather than brown. Also, you can roast different vegetables together if their cooking times are similar, so mix it up!

Vegetable Roasting Times

VEGETABLES	HOW TO CUT	ROASTING TIME AT 450°F	GARNISH & SERVING
Asparagus	Trim	10 to 15 minutes	Garnish with 1 teaspoon freshly grated lemon
Beets (without tops)	Whole, unpeeled, pricked with a fork, then peeled after roasting 1 hour	roasting 1 hour	Chop, season with salt, pepper, and 1 teaspoon freshly grated orange peel
Broccoli	Trim and peel stem, split florets into 1½-inch-wide pieces	10 to 15 minutes	Sprinkle with 1 tablespoon grated Cheddar
Brussels Sprouts	Trim and halve through stem end 15 to 20 minutes	15 to 20 minutes	Season with salt and pepper, serve immediately
Butternut Squash	2-inch pieces	40 minutes	Toss with ½ teaspoon dried rosemary, crumbled, before roasting
Carrots	1-inch pieces	30 to 40 minutes	Toss with 1/2 teaspoon pumpkin pie spice
Cauliflower	1½-inch florets	20 to 30 minutes	Sprinkle with 2 tablespoons chopped fresh parsley
Eggplant	½ -inch-thick slices	20 to 25 minutes	Drizzle with 1 tablespoon extra-virgin olive oil
Green Beans	Trim	20 to 30 minutes	Toss with 2 tablespoons each lemon juice and chopped fresh dill
Onions	Cut into wedges	20 to 30 minutes	Remove onions from oven and brush with mixture of 1 tablespoon brown sugar, 1 teaspoon apple cider vinegar. Return to oven and roast for 5 more minutes
Potatoes	2-inch pieces	45 minutes	Garnish with ½ freshly grated orange peel
Sweet Peppers	1-inch-wide strips	30 minutes	Garnish with 3 basil leaves, thinly sliced
Sweet Potatoes	Cut crosswise in half, then lengthwise into 1-inch wedges	30 minutes	Toss with 2 tablespoons fresh chopped rosemary before roasting
Turnips	Peel and cut into 6 wedges	45 to 50 minutes	Garnish with 1 tablespoon chopped fresh mint
Zucchini	Trim and cut in half crosswise then each half quartered	15 to 20 minutes	Garnish with 1 tablespoon freshly grated Parmesan

Roasted Jerk Chicken
(page 42)

1 Chicken

There are not many dishes that compare to roast chicken. When cooked on a sheet pan, chicken stands up to the high temperatures of the oven and comes out with crispy skin and juicy meat. Whether tossed with some vegetables in Rustic Smoky Glazed Chicken & Veggie Bake or as a topping in Buffalo Chicken & Ranch Pizza or even as a light meal in Autumn Chicken & Squash Salad, chicken is always a crowd-pleaser and quick weeknight dinner solution.

Spanish Chicken &
PEPPERS

This chicken meal is easy to assemble and also makes
a delicious sandwich.

ACTIVE TIME: 10 MINUTES   **TOTAL TIME:** 45 MINUTES
MAKES: 4 SERVINGS

2½ pounds assorted small chicken parts
     (cut breasts into halves)

1   pound mini sweet peppers

1½ tablespoons olive oil

Salt

Freshly ground black pepper

½   cup light mayonnaise

1   clove garlic, pressed

½   teaspoon smoked paprika

Baguette, for serving

1 Preheat oven to 450°F. In a large bowl, toss
chicken and peppers with oil and ½ teaspoon
each salt and pepper. Arrange chicken and
vegetables on a baking sheet. Roast in oven for
35 minutes, or until chicken is cooked through
(165°F).

2 While the chicken and vegetables cook, stir
together mayonnaise, garlic, and smoked paprika
in a small bowl. Serve chicken and peppers on a
baguette with garlic mayo.

EACH SERVING: ABOUT 500 CALORIES, 39G PROTEIN,
10G CARBOHYDRATE, 34G TOTAL FAT (7G SATURATED),
2G FIBER, 595MG SODIUM.

TIP

Serve the chicken and peppers with your
favorite rice and black beans for a meal
alternative.

Rustic Smoky Glazed Chicken &
VEGGIE BAKE

Roast spice-rubbed chicken and veggies for a hearty meal.
The veggies come out caramelized and tastier than you can imagine.
For photo, see page 2.

ACTIVE TIME: 10 MINUTES   **TOTAL TIME:** 50 MINUTES
MAKES: 6 SERVINGS

2   teaspoons smoked paprika

2   teaspoons ground cumin

Freshly ground black pepper

Extra-virgin olive oil

Salt

1   pound potatoes

1   pound carrots

2   pounds Brussels sprouts

2   pounds onion, cut into quarters

2   pounds halved mushrooms

2   pounds asparagus, cut in thirds

2   pounds whole green or yellow beans

1½ pounds chicken pieces

Chopped parsley, for serving

Lemon wedges, for serving

1   Preheat oven to 450°F. In a small bowl, combine smoked paprika, cumin, and ½ teaspoon pepper to make a rub.

2   On a large rimmed baking sheet, toss potatoes, carrots, Brussels sprouts, and onions with 2 tablespoons oil, one-third of rub, and ½ teaspoon salt. Roast the vegetables in the oven for 10 minutes.

3   On another baking sheet, toss mushrooms, asparagus, and green beans with 2 teaspoons oil and one-third of rub. Push the vegetables to one side of the pan. On other side, arrange chicken pieces. Sprinkle with remaining rub. Season vegetables and chicken with ½ teaspoon salt. Place baking sheet with chicken in the oven. Roast both pans for 20 to 35 minutes, or until chicken is cooked and all vegetables are softened. Transfer chicken from pan to platter if cooked before vegetables are tender.

EACH SERVING: ABOUT 270 CALORIES, 18G PROTEIN, 23G CARBOHYDRATE, 13G TOTAL FAT (3G SATURATED), 5G FIBER, 440MG SODIUM.

TIP

Swap winter vegetables like Brussels sprouts and mushrooms in the summertime for zucchini, grape tomatoes, and bell pepper.

Buffalo Chicken &
RANCH PIZZA

These grandma-style slices bake on a sheet pan, so everyone gets his or her favorite piece—from extra-crusty corners to topping-loaded middles.

ACTIVE TIME: 15 MINUTES   **TOTAL TIME:** 50 MINUTES PLUS DOUGH RISING
MAKES: 8 SERVINGS

PIZZA

Easy Homemade Dough, or 1½-pound ball pizzeria dough

3/4 cup part-skim ricotta cheese

1/4 cup ranch dressing

1/2 cup hot sauce

3 tablespoons unsalted butter, melted

1 tablespoon white (distilled) vinegar

3 cups (about 12 ounces) shredded rotisserie chicken

2 ounces blue cheese, crumbled

Thinly sliced green onions, for garnish

EASY HOMEMADE DOUGH

3½ cups all-purpose flour

3 tablespoons, plus 1/4 cup extra-virgin olive oil

Salt

1¼ teaspoons instant yeast

1 Preheat oven to 475°F. In a medium bowl, combine ricotta and ranch dressing. Spread ricotta mixture over the dough. Bake the dough for 15 minutes.
2 Meanwhile, in medium bowl, whisk together hot sauce, butter, and vinegar. Add chicken and toss to coat. Remove dough from oven after 15 minutes and scatter chicken over ricotta mixture. Top the pizza with blue cheese.

3 Bake in the oven for an additional 20 to 25 minutes, or until bottom of crust is golden brown. Garnish with green onions before serving.

....

EACH SERVING: ABOUT 495 CALORIES, 17G PROTEIN, 46G CARBOHYDRATE, 29G TOTAL FAT (9G SATURATED), 2G FIBER, 1,245MG SODIUM.

EASY HOMEMADE DOUGH

In stand mixer with paddle attachment, mix flour, 3 tablespoons oil, 1½ teaspoons salt, and yeast on low speed until combined. Add 1½ cups lukewarm water. Mix on medium 1 minute. Increase speed to medium-high and mix 5 minutes. Meanwhile, brush 1/4 cup of oil on the bottom and sides of an 18 x 12-inch light-colored rimmed baking sheet. Pour dough onto oiled sheet and rub with excess oil until evenly coated. Gently stretch the dough to fill most of baking sheet. Cover with plastic wrap; let stand in warm spot for two hours. Remove plastic. With hands, stretch and push dough until it covers bottom of pan.

TIP

Buy fresh dough from your local pizzeria. It will save time since the dough will not need to rise before topping with your favorite ingredients.

BBQ Chicken
PIZZA

This fast, weeknight-friendly tortilla pizza features beloved barbecue flavors, so you can savor the summer all year long.

ACTIVE TIME: 10 MINUTES   **TOTAL TIME:** 25 MINUTES
MAKES: 4 SERVINGS

4   flour tortillas

2   cups chopped rotisserie chicken

½   cup barbecue sauce

1   cup corn

½   cup finely chopped red onion

1   small orange pepper

¾   cup shredded smoked mozzarella

¼   cup chopped cilantro

1 Arrange oven racks in top and bottom thirds of oven. Preheat oven to 475°F. Spray two baking sheets with nonstick cooking spray; place 2 tortillas on each baking sheet.

2 Toss chopped rotisserie chicken with barbecue sauce. Divide among tortillas. Top with corn, red onion, orange pepper, and shredded smoked mozzarella.

3 Bake 12 minutes, or until tortillas are crisp around edges, switching racks halfway through cooking. Top with chopped cilantro.

EACH SERVING: ABOUT 500 CALORIES, 34G PROTEIN, 51G CARBOHYDRATE, 18G TOTAL FAT (8G SATURATED), 3G FIBER, 1,370MG SODIUM.

TIP

Bump up the fiber in this meal by using whole wheat wraps as the pizza base.

Cilantro-Lime Chicken
WITH SPICE-ROASTED CARROTS

This chicken dinner is spiced with classic Latin flavors like cilantro and lime, and it gets an Asian kick from soy sauce and ginger.

ACTIVE TIME: 35 MINUTES   **TOTAL TIME:** 1 HOUR 20 MINUTES PLUS MARINATING
MAKES: 6 SERVINGS

1   cup fresh cilantro leaves, packed

1   cup fresh mint leaves, packed

¼   cup fresh tarragon leaves, packed

½   cup olive oil

⅓   cup soy sauce

¼   cup lime juice

3   tablespoons cider vinegar

5   cloves garlic

1   jalapeño, sliced

2   tablespoons chopped peeled fresh ginger

1   teaspoon dried oregano

1   teaspoon ground cumin

Salt

3   pounds assorted chicken parts like thighs, drumsticks, and wings

⅓   cup mayonnaise

SPICE-ROASTED CARROTS

1 ½   pounds medium carrots, quartered lengthwise

2   tablespoons olive oil

1   teaspoon ground cumin

½   teaspoon smoked paprika

Salt

Freshly ground black pepper

1 In food processor, puree herbs with oil, soy sauce, lime juice, vinegar, garlic, jalapeño, ginger, oregano, cumin, and 1 teaspoon salt until smooth. Transfer ¾ cup to small bowl; set aside. Transfer remaining marinade to gallon-size plastic bag and add chicken. Seal bag and toss to coat. Refrigerate and marinate chicken for at least 5 hours or up to overnight.

2 Preheat oven to 375°F. Line a baking sheet with foil and place a wired rack on top. Arrange chicken on rack. Discard leftover marinade in plastic bag. Place the baking sheet with chicken in the oven and bake 30 minutes.

3 After 30 minutes, increase the oven temperature to 450°F. Roast chicken for another 15 to 20 minutes, or until chicken is cooked through (165°F).

4 While the chicken roasts, whisk together reserved marinade and mayonnaise in a small bowl. Set green sauce aside. Serve chicken with green sauce and Spice-Roasted Carrots.

5 **Prepare Spice-Roasted Carrots:** In a large bowl, toss the carrots with oil, cumin, paprika, and ½ teaspoon each salt and pepper. Transfer to a rimmed baking sheet and distribute evenly. Roast carrots in 450°F oven for 30 minutes, or until tender, stirring twice.

EACH SERVING (WITHOUT THE CARROTS): ABOUT 500 CALORIES, 32G PROTEIN, 4G CARBOHYDRATE, 39G TOTAL FAT (8G SATURATED), 1G FIBER, 1,140MG SODIUM.

Honey Mustard–Glazed
CHICKEN BAKE

You can make this sweet glaze a day ahead of time. When it comes time to get cooking, it's just a quick pop in the oven to chicken perfection.

ACTIVE TIME: 25 MINUTES   **TOTAL TIME:** 1 HOUR
MAKES: 4 SERVINGS

1   pound parsnips, sliced on an angle

1   pound Yukon Gold potatoes, scrubbed and quartered

½   pound carrots, quartered lengthwise, then cut into 2-inch pieces

1   medium red onion, cut into 8 wedges

2   tablespoons olive oil

5   sprigs fresh thyme

Salt

4   chicken thighs

4   chicken drumsticks

Freshly ground black pepper

3   tablespoons Dijon mustard

2   tablespoons whole-grain mustard

2   tablespoons honey

1   tablespoon brown sugar

1   Preheat oven to 425°F. On a large baking sheet, toss parsnips, potatoes, carrots, onion, oil, thyme, and ½ teaspoon salt. Place baking sheet in oven and roast vegetables for 15 minutes.

2   Remove baking sheet from oven. Arrange chicken pieces in a single layer over vegetables. Sprinkle with ½ teaspoon salt and ¼ teaspoon pepper. Return baking sheet to oven and roast for 15 minutes.

3   In medium bowl, whisk together Dijon mustard, whole-grain mustard, honey, and brown sugar. After 15 minutes, remove baking sheet from oven. Drizzle mustard mixture over chicken and vegetables. Return baking sheet to oven and roast for 25 minutes, or until chicken is cooked through (165°F) and vegetables are tender. Serve chicken with vegetables.

EACH SERVING: ABOUT 760 CALORIES, 42G PROTEIN, 60G CARBOHYDRATE, 38G TOTAL FAT (9G SATURATED), 8G FIBER, 1,105MG SODIUM.

TIP

Prepare potatoes ahead of time to save time when preparing this meal. To prevent them from browning, cover potato pieces with cold water and juice from half of a lemon. Store in the refrigerator for up to 1 day. Before roasting the potatoes, drain the water and pat them dry.

Chicken with Caramelized
CAULIFLOWER & GREEN OLIVES

Cauliflower gains incredible flavor when roasted. Paired with a homemade pesto-like sauce with olives, almonds, and parsley, this healthy chicken dish offers many complex flavors.

ACTIVE TIME: 10 MINUTES   **TOTAL TIME:** 50 MINUTES
MAKES: 4 SERVINGS

1   head cauliflower

Extra-virgin olive oil

Salt

Freshly ground black pepper

1   pound chicken breast tenders

1   teaspoon freshly grated lemon peel

1/4   cup slivered almonds

1/3   cup pitted green olives

1/4   cup packed fresh flat-leaf parsley

1   Preheat oven to 450°F. In 18 x 12-inch jelly-roll pan, mix cauliflower, 2 teaspoons oil, 1/8 teaspoon each salt and pepper. Spread cauliflower in single layer. Roast cauliflower in the oven for 20 to 25 minutes, or until golden brown.

2   While cauliflower roasts, in large bowl, combine chicken, lemon peel, 1 teaspoon oil, 1/4 teaspoon each salt and pepper. Remove pan from oven and push cauliflower to one side of pan. On the other side, arrange chicken in a single layer. Return pan to oven and roast for 10 minutes, or until chicken is cooked through (165°F).

3   Meanwhile, add almonds to a food processor, pulse until finely ground. Add olives and parsley and pulse until smooth. With machine running, add 1 tablespoon oil until it's fully incorporated, scraping sides of bowl as needed.

4   While chicken and cauliflower are still hot, add sauce from food processor and stir until well combined. Transfer to serving plates and garnish with additional parsley.

EACH SERVING: ABOUT 360 CALORIES, 45G PROTEIN, 12G CARBOHYDRATE, 15G TOTAL FAT (2G SATURATED), 6G FIBER, 660MG SODIUM.

Roasted Chicken Pieces
WITH PEARS & GREEN ONIONS

This kid-friendly recipe couldn't be simpler to prepare—
just sprinkle chicken pieces and sliced pears with lemon zest
and green onions and roast until golden and tender.

ACTIVE TIME: 15 MINUTES   **TOTAL TIME:** 45 MINUTES
MAKES: 4 SERVINGS

2   lemons

1   bunch green onions

2   tablespoons olive oil

Salt

Freshly ground black pepper

1   (4 pound) cut-up chicken (8 pieces),
     skin removed from all but wings

3   Bosc pears

1 Preheat oven to 450°F. Spray 15½ x 10½-inch jelly-roll pan with nonstick cooking spray.

2 From 1 lemon, grate 2 teaspoons peel and squeeze 1 tablespoon juice. Cut remaining lemon into wedges. Cut white and light-green portion of green onions into 2-inch pieces; thinly slice dark-green tops. Set aside lemon juice, lemon wedges, and sliced green onion tops.

3 In large bowl, stir together lemon peel, oil, ¾ teaspoon salt, and ½ teaspoon pepper. Add chicken, pears, and white and light-green onion pieces, and toss until coated.

4 Arrange chicken mixture in prepared pan. Roast 30 to 35 minutes, or until juices run clear when thickest part of chicken is pierced with tip of knife and pears are fork-tender. Transfer chicken mixture to warm platter; drizzle with lemon juice, and sprinkle with green onion tops. Serve with pan juices and lemon wedges.

EACH SERVING: ABOUT 375 CALORIES, 44G PROTEIN, 20G CARBOHYDRATE, 14G TOTAL FAT (3G SATURATED), 4G FIBER, 595MG SODIUM.

Pancetta
CHICKEN

Wrapped in salty pancetta, this baked chicken will be juicy
with a super crispy texture.

ACTIVE TIME: 5 MINUTES   **TOTAL TIME:** 45 MINUTES
MAKES: 4 SERVINGS

1½ **pounds small skinless, boneless
chicken-breast halves**

Salt

Freshly ground black pepper

Thinly sliced pancetta

1 **pound green beans**

2 **tablespoons extra-virgin olive oil**

Lemon wedges, for serving

1 Preheat oven to 450°F. Sprinkle chicken-
breast halves with ½ teaspoon salt. Wrap 2 slices
of pancetta over each chicken breast and tuck
pancetta ends underneath. Season with pepper.
Place on foil-lined rimmed baking sheet.

2 On another baking sheet, toss green beans
with oil; season with salt and pepper. Place
baking sheets in oven, and roast chicken
and vegetables for 30 minutes, or until chicken
is cooked through (165°F). Serve chicken and
green beans together with lemon wedges.

EACH SERVING: ABOUT 265 CALORIES, 38G PROTEIN,
10G CARBOHYDRATE, 8G TOTAL FAT (2G SATURATED),
4G FIBER, 520MG SODIUM.

Rosemary-Lemon
ROAST CHICKEN

Every would-be Julia Child needs a roast-chicken dish in her cooking repertoire. This simple dinner will always impress.

ACTIVE TIME: 10 MINUTES   **TOTAL TIME:** 40 MINUTES
MAKES: 4 SERVINGS

1   pound carrots, cut into 2-inch lengths

1   pound fennel bulbs, trimmed and thinly sliced

2   tablespoons olive oil

Salt

8   small chicken pieces (drumsticks and thighs)

Lemons

2   tablespoons loosely packed rosemary leaves

Freshly ground black pepper

1 Preheat oven to 475°F. In a large roasting pan or rimmed baking sheet, toss carrots and fennel with oil and ¼ teaspoon salt; spread in single layer. Arrange chicken pieces, patted dry, on top of vegetables.

2 Zest lemons over the chicken, and season chicken with rosemary leaves and ½ teaspoon each salt and pepper. Thinly slice lemons and place on top of chicken.

3 Roast 30 minutes, or until vegetables are tender and chicken is cooked through (165°F).

EACH SERVING: ABOUT 685 CALORIES, 58G PROTEIN, 20G CARBOHYDRATE, 41G TOTAL FAT (10G SATURATED), 7G FIBER, 824MG SODIUM.

TIP

Shave calories and fat off this meal by removing the chicken skin before eating. By cooking the bird with the skin on, it preserves its juices and flavorful taste.

Mahogany Chicken &
BROCCOLI

"Mahogany" here refers to a mix of soy and honey that gives
a dish's glaze its rich color and caramelized flavor.
Try this glaze on pork tenderloin, too!

ACTIVE TIME: 10 MINUTES   **TOTAL TIME:** 40 MINUTES
MAKES: 4 SERVINGS

2   tablespoons lower-sodium soy sauce

2   tablespoons honey

2   cloves garlic, pressed

2   teaspoons peeled and grated fresh ginger

1½ pounds chicken thighs, fat trimmed

1   bunch green onions, chopped

1   pound broccoli florets

2   tablespoons vegetable oil

Salt

1 Preheat oven to 450°F. Line two rimmed baking sheets with foil. In large bowl, whisk together soy sauce, honey, garlic, and ginger. Add chicken thighs and green onions; toss to coat.

2 Arrange chicken, skin side up, and green onions on a prepared baking sheet. On another prepared baking sheet, toss broccoli florets with vegetable oil and ⅛ teaspoon salt; arrange in single layer.

3 Roast chicken and broccoli in 450°F oven for 30 minutes, or until chicken is cooked through (165°F) and broccoli is tender.

EACH SERVING: ABOUT 380 CALORIES, 28G PROTEIN, 19G CARBOHYDRATE, 22G TOTAL FAT (5G SATURATED), 4G FIBER, 485MG SODIUM.

Light Chicken
PARMESAN

Eat this recipe when you're craving the high-calorie Italian classic.

ACTIVE TIME: 10 MINUTES   **TOTAL TIME:** 25 MINUTES
MAKES: 4 SERVINGS

¼ cup Italian-style bread crumbs

¼ cup grated Parmesan

4   thin-sliced chicken-breast cutlets
    (about 1 pound)

Salt

1   pint grape tomatoes, cut in halves

2   ounces part-skim mozzarella, shredded

5   ounces arugula

1   tablespoon red wine vinegar

1   teaspoon extra-virgin olive oil

1 Preheat oven to 425°F. Combine Italian-style bread crumbs and grated Parmesan. Arrange chicken breasts on foil-lined baking sheet; sprinkle tops with ¼ teaspoon salt, then with crumbs, pressing to adhere. Arrange tomatoes around chicken; spray with nonstick cooking spray. Bake at 425°F for 15 minutes.

2 Sprinkle cutlets with mozzarella; bake until cheese melts. Toss tomatoes with arugula, vinegar, oil, and ¼ teaspoon salt. Serve salad with chicken.

EACH SERVING: ABOUT 270 CALORIES, 31G PROTEIN, 15G CARBOHYDRATE, 9G TOTAL FAT (4G SATURATED), 2G FIBER, 860MG SODIUM.

Crunchy
DEVILED CHICKEN

Boost the flavor in breaded chicken by adding spicy brown mustard and smoked paprika to the dredging process.

ACTIVE TIME: 10 MINUTES **TOTAL TIME:** 30 MINUTES
MAKES: 4 SERVINGS

3   tablespoons spicy brown mustard

1   large egg

½   teaspoon smoked paprika

1¼ pounds skinless, boneless chicken thighs

1¼ cups panko bread crumbs

1   pound medium carrots, halved lengthwise

Salt

Parsley, for garnish

Greens, for serving

1 Spray two rimmed baking sheets with nonstick cooking spray. Whisk together mustard, egg, and smoked paprika. Dip chicken thighs in egg mixture, then dredge through panko, pressing to adhere. Place on one prepared sheet.

2 On other sheet, arrange carrots. Spray chicken and carrots with nonstick cooking spray; sprinkle with ½ teaspoon salt. Bake at 450°F for 20 minutes, or until carrots are tender and chicken is cooked through (165°F).

3 Garnish with parsley. Serve over greens.

EACH SERVING: ABOUT 355 CALORIES, 30G PROTEIN, 31G CARBOHYDRATE, 10G TOTAL FAT (3G SATURATED), 4G FIBER, 605MG SODIUM.

TIP

If you wish to dress your salad, combine lemon juice and olive oil for a simple dressing.

Baked
FRIED CHICKEN

This oven-fried chicken is a healthier version of the classic meal
with a light and tasty coating.

ACTIVE TIME: 10 MINUTES   **TOTAL TIME:** 45 MINUTES
MAKES: 4 SERVINGS

½ cup plain dried bread crumbs

¼ cup grated Parmesan cheese

2 tablespoons cornmeal

½ teaspoon ground red pepper

1 egg white

Salt

1 chicken, cut into pieces

Green onions, for garnish

1 Preheat oven to 425°F. Spray 15½ x 10½-inch jelly-roll pan with nonstick cooking spray.

2 On waxed paper, mix bread crumbs, cheese, cornmeal, and ground red pepper. In pie plate, beat egg white and ½ teaspoon salt.

3 Dip each piece of chicken in egg-white mixture, then coat with bread-crumb mixture. Place chicken in pan; spray lightly with cooking spray.

4 Bake chicken 35 minutes, or until coating is crisp and juices run clear when chicken is pierced with tip of knife. Garnish with green onions if you like.

EACH SERVING: ABOUT 480 CALORIES, 48G PROTEIN, 15G CARBOHYDRATE, 24G TOTAL FAT (7G SATURATED), 1G FIBER, 624MG SODIUM.

Almond-Crusted Chicken
WITH RAINBOW SLAW

The colorful, crunchy slaw combines carrots, red cabbage, oranges, and yellow peppers in a refreshing, immune-supporting side.

ACTIVE TIME: 20 MINUTES   **TOTAL TIME:** 30 MINUTES
MAKES: 4 SERVINGS

2   medium oranges

4   cups red cabbage

2   large carrots

1   large yellow pepper

2   tablespoons chives, chopped

3   tablespoons white wine vinegar

Canola oil

Salt

Freshly ground black pepper

1   tablespoon all-purpose flour

½   cup almonds

1   large egg white

¼   teaspoon ground cumin

¼   teaspoon no-salt-added chili powder

4   skinless, boneless chicken-breast cutlets

1 Arrange one oven rack in lowest position; place 15½ x 10½-inch jelly-roll pan on rack. Preheat oven to 450°F.

2 Peel the skin and white pith from the oranges; discard. Cut oranges into segments over a large bowl to catch excess juice. Add cabbage, carrots, yellow pepper, chives, vinegar, 1 teaspoon oil, and ¼ teaspoon each salt and pepper to large bowl. Toss slaw and set aside.

3 Spread flour evenly on a medium plate. On another plate spread the almonds. In pie plate, beat egg white until foamy.

4 In a small bowl combine cumin, chili powder, and ¼ teaspoon each salt and pepper. Sprinkle seasoning mixture on each chicken breast. Press one side of chicken breast in the flour and shake off excess flour. Dip the same side in egg white. Then, press the same side into the almonds. Repeat with remaining chicken breasts.

5 Remove hot baking sheet from the oven and brush with 3 teaspoons oil. Place the chicken on the baking sheet with the almond crust side down. Roast chicken on the lowest rack for 10 to 12 minutes (165°F). Serve chicken breasts with slaw.

EACH SERVING: ABOUT 350 CALORIES, 30G PROTEIN, 28G CARBOHYDRATE, 15G TOTAL FAT (2G SATURATED), 7G FIBER, 425MG SODIUM.

TIP

Chopped almonds are chockful of healthy fats that keep skin supple and protein that helps keep you full.

Autumn Chicken &
SQUASH SALAD

Make this dish on the weekend and double the recipe
for a delightful lunch throughout the week.

ACTIVE TIME: 10 MINUTES   **TOTAL TIME:** 50 MINUTES
MAKES: 4 SERVINGS

2 (20-ounce) containers of butternut squash, chopped

1 pound skinless, boneless chicken thighs

2 tablespoons olive oil

Salt

Freshly ground black pepper

5 ounces mixed greens

3 tablespoons lemon juice

4 ounces goat cheese, crumbled

1 Preheat oven to 425°F. On two large rimmed baking sheets, toss butternut squash and chicken thighs with oil and ½ teaspoon each salt and pepper. Bake in the oven for 40 minutes, or until squash is tender. Remove baking sheets from oven and let cool. Then chop the chicken. In a large bowl toss the chicken with the squash, along with mixed greens, lemon juice, and goat cheese. Season to taste with salt and pepper and serve.

EACH SERVING: ABOUT 385 CALORIES, 28G PROTEIN, 28G CARBOHYDRATE, 20G TOTAL FAT (7G SATURATED), 9G FIBER , 555MG SODIUM.

TIP

For a sweet addition, add roasted pears. Cut two pears in chunks and add to the baking sheets.

Sweet & Sticky Chicken
WITH SNOW PEAS

Hoisin, both sweet and salty, is a thick pungent sauce
often used in Chinese cuisine.

ACTIVE TIME: 5 MINUTES   **TOTAL TIME:** 50 MINUTES
MAKES: 4 SERVINGS

2½ pounds chicken drumsticks and thighs

¼   cup hoisin sauce

Salt

Freshly ground black pepper

1   pound snow peas

½   teaspoon crushed red pepper flakes

2   teaspoons toasted sesame oil

Chopped cilantro, for garnish

1 Preheat oven to 450°F. In a large bowl, toss
chicken with hoisin sauce, ½ teaspoon each salt
and pepper. Arrange chicken on a foil-lined
rimmed baking sheet. Roast in the oven for
30 minutes, or until cooked through (165°F).
2 While the chicken roasts, boil snow peas for
5 minutes, or until tender. Drain and then toss
with red pepper flakes, sesame oil, and a pinch
of salt.
3 Serve chicken over snow peas. Garnish with
cilantro.

EACH SERVING: ABOUT 370 CALORIES, 38G PROTEIN,
16G CARBOHYDRATE, 16G TOTAL FAT (4G SATURATED),
4G FIBER, 680MG SODIUM.

The Best Way to Roast a Chicken

While roast chicken can be so simple—and great to have in your dinner repertoire on cold, wintry nights—it seems that roast-chicken nirvana lies just beyond the grasp of many home cooks. Here are a few tips to take your chicken to the next level:

1. For better browning and crisping, start at a moderate heat.

Begin cooking the chicken at about 375°F, until the breast meat is roughly 125°F (about 40 minutes for a 5-pound chicken). Then raise the temperature to 475°F and blast it for the last 20 minutes or until the breast meat reaches 165°F. For extra color, broil it on high for a couple of minutes.

2. Season the bird.

Chicken is a mild bird; even the highest-quality chickens are still fairly tame in flavor. Use your seasonings liberally, particularly on the breasts, which have a much lower ratio of skin to meat than the thighs and drumsticks.

3. Switch up your seasonings.

Butter, garlic, herbs, and lemon create a classic, but consider switching it up! Instead, rub the bird with a mixture of chili powder, lime zest, lime juice, cumin, brown sugar, and cayenne for a frisky flavor profile.

4. Do not cover with foil once your chicken is out of the oven.

Covering the chicken immediately ends up steaming the skin. Instead, let the chicken rest, exposed, for 10 minutes before serving.

Another Option: Spatchcock your chicken.

By using this technique, the chicken will cook faster and the skin will crisp better. It also ensures even cooking time between the breast and dark meat.

Here's how to do it: Starting with a whole bird, take any innards out from the cavity and discard them. Flip the bird onto its breast. With a sturdy pair of kitchen scissors, cut from tail to neck just to the left, then just to the right of the backbone to remove it. Discard the backbone or save it for chicken stock. Flip it back to breast side up and push down on it to flatten. That's it!

Roasted Chicken
WITH WINTER VEGETABLES

Roasting turnips, fennel, and potatoes with a whole chicken
gives these winter vegetables incredible flavor.

ACTIVE TIME: 15 MINUTES **TOTAL TIME:** 1 HOUR
MAKES: 4 SERVINGS

1   large onion, sliced

1   pound baby red potatoes, cut into quarters

4   large carrots, cut into thirds

2   small turnips, cut into wedges

1   small fennel bulb, cut into wedges

8   sprigs fresh thyme, plus additional
    for garnish

7   cloves garlic, crushed

Olive oil

Salt

Freshly ground black pepper

1   whole chicken (about 3½ pounds)

1 Preheat oven to 450°F. In 18 x 12-inch jelly-roll pan, arrange onion slices in single layer in center. In large bowl, toss potatoes, carrots, turnips, fennel, 4 thyme sprigs, 3 garlic cloves, 1 tablespoon oil, ¼ teaspoon each salt and pepper until well mixed. Spread in even layer around onion slices in pan.

2 If necessary, remove bag with giblets and neck from chicken cavity; discard or reserve for another use. Rub chicken cavity with ¼ teaspoon each salt and pepper. Place remaining 4 thyme sprigs and 4 garlic cloves in cavity and tie legs together with kitchen string. Rub 1 teaspoon oil on chicken and sprinkle with ⅛ teaspoon each salt and pepper.

3 Place chicken, breast side up, on onion slices in pan. Roast 45 minutes, or until juices run clear when thickest part of thigh is pierced with tip of knife and temperature on meat thermometer inserted into thickest part of thigh reaches 175°F. Let chicken stand on pan 10 minutes to set juices for easier carving. Meanwhile, transfer vegetables around chicken to serving platter, leaving space in center for chicken. Transfer chicken and onion to serving platter with vegetables, tilting chicken slightly as you lift to allow any juices inside to run into pan. Skim and discard fat from juices in pan; pour into small bowl and serve with chicken. Garnish with additional thyme sprigs.

EACH SERVING: ABOUT 555 CALORIES, 45G PROTEIN, 37G CARBOHYDRATE, 25G TOTAL FAT (6G SATURATED), 7G FIBER, 405MG SODIUM.

Roasted JERK CHICKEN

Dig into this juicy, roasted jerk chicken with
black beans and rice served on the side. For photo, see page 10.

ACTIVE TIME: 15 MINUTES   **TOTAL TIME:** 1 HOUR 30 MINUTES
MAKES: 4 SERVINGS

2   green onions, sliced

2   cloves garlic

1   jalapeños, sliced

2   tablespoons canola oil

1½ tablespoons fresh lime juice

1½ tablespoons soy sauce

1   tablespoon brown sugar

¼   teaspoon ground allspice

Salt

Freshly ground black pepper

1   whole chicken (about 4 pounds)

1 Preheat oven to 425°F. Line large rimmed baking sheet with foil; place rack on foil.

2 In blender or food processor, blend green onions, garlic, jalapeño, oil, lime juice, soy sauce, brown sugar, allspice, ½ teaspoon salt, and ¼ teaspoon pepper until smooth.

3 Arrange the chicken on rack. With hands, gently loosen chicken skin from meat. Spoon some green onion mixture into cavity of chicken and under skin; rub remaining all over outside of chicken. Tuck wings behind breast and tie drumsticks together with butcher's twine. Roast 1 hour.

4 Reduce oven temperature to 375°F. Roast another 15 minutes, or until chicken is cooked through (165°F). Serve chicken.

EACH SERVING: ABOUT 600 CALORIES, 60G PROTEIN, 5G CARBOHYDRATE, 36G TOTAL FAT (9G SATURATED), 0G FIBER, 395MG SODIUM.

TIP

Leftover chicken can be used to make a banh mi sandwich. Assemble chicken, shredded carrots, sliced cucumbers, and cilantro leaves on a roll with mayonnaise.

Spicy DRUMSTICKS

Get out of your weeknight chicken rut with
these fiery, glazed drumsticks.

ACTIVE TIME: 5 MINUTES   TOTAL TIME: 50 MINUTES
MAKES: 4 SERVINGS

¼ cup olive oil

¼ cup soy sauce

3 tablespoons lime juice

3 tablespoons brown sugar

5 thin slices peeled fresh ginger

3 green onions, sliced

2 cloves garlic

3 jalapeños or 1 habañero chile

5 sprigs fresh thyme

¼ teaspoon ground allspice

Salt

12 chicken drumsticks

Sliced jalapeños and lime wedges, for garnish

1 In blender, puree oil, soy sauce, lime juice, brown sugar, ginger, green onions, garlic, jalapeños or hanañero, thyme, allspice, and ¾ teaspoon salt until smooth; transfer sauce to a gallon-size resealable bag. Add the chicken drumsticks to the bag and seal the bag, removing excess air. Toss to coat the chicken; place the bag on large plate. Refrigerate for at least 4 hours or up to overnight.

2 When ready to cook, preheat oven to 425°F. Line a large rimmed baking sheet with foil and fit a rack into the baking sheet. Then, remove the drumsticks from the marinade. Discard excess marinade and plastic bag. Gently pat dry each drumstick and then arrange the drumsticks on the rack, spacing them 1 inch apart. Roast for 35 to 40 minutes, or until cooked through (160°F). To serve, garnish with jalapeños and lime wedges, if desired.

EACH SERVING: ABOUT 195 CALORIES, 21G PROTEIN, 2G CARBOHYDRATE, 11G TOTAL FAT (3G SATURATED), 0G FIBER, 30MG SODIUM.

TIP

Complete this cozy meal with a side of coconut rice and black-eyed peas.

Meatball-Mozzarella Pizza
(page 54)

2 | Meats

Other meats—like beef, lamb, and pork—also perform well when transformed in the oven. Whether shaped in meatloaves like in Gochujang-Glazed Meatloaf with Green Beans or formed into meatballs in Greek-Style Meatballs, baking these meals eliminates the extra fat added with other cooking methods like frying. With a golden browned exterior, Roast Pork with Winter Veggies and Pork Tenderloin with Roasted-Lemon Orzo gain depths of flavor in 30 minutes.

Mustard-Crusted Mini Meatloaves
WITH ROASTED APPLES

Grated zucchini lightens this meatloaf recipe
and adds nutrients.

ACTIVE TIME: 10 MINUTES   **TOTAL TIME:** 40 MINUTES
MAKES: 4 SERVINGS

1¼ pounds ground beef or turkey

1   small zucchini, grated

⅓   cup seasoned bread crumbs

Salt

Freshly ground black pepper

2   tablespoons Dijon mustard

3   small Gala or Empire apples, cored
     and cut into 8 wedges

1   teaspoon fresh rosemary, chopped

¼   teaspoon cayenne pepper

1   tablespoon extra-virgin olive oil

Snipped chives, for garnish

1 Preheat oven to 425°F. In large bowl, combine ground meat, zucchini, bread crumbs, and ½ teaspoon each salt and pepper. Form meat mixture into 4 meatloaves and place on foil-lined rimmed baking sheet; brush the tops of each mini meatloaf with Dijon.

2 In another bowl, toss apple wedges with rosemary, cayenne, oil, and a pinch of salt. Arrange the apples around the meatloaves. Bake in the oven for 30 minutes, or until loaves are cooked through (165°F). Before serving, garnish with chives.

....

EACH SERVING: ABOUT 420 CALORIES, 32G PROTEIN, 24G CARBOHYDRATE, 20G TOTAL FAT (7G SATURATED), 4G FIBER, 665MG SODIUM.

Gochujang-Glazed Meatloaf
WITH GREEN BEANS

Gochujang, a Korean chili sauce, is the ideal blend of sweet, savory, and sour. Plus, unlike other hot sauces, it won't burn your mouth.

ACTIVE TIME: 10 MINUTES   **TOTAL TIME:** 1 HOUR 5 MINUTES
MAKES: 8 SERVINGS

1   pound ground beef

1   pound ground pork

1   small onion, grated

6   saltines, finely crushed

½   cup packed fresh mint, chopped

9   tablespoons gochujang, divided

1   large egg

Salt

4   tablespoons olive oil

2   teaspoons ground coriander

2   pounds green beans, trimmed

¼   cup ketchup

1   Preheat oven to 425°F. Line a baking sheet with foil. In a large bowl, mix together beef, pork, onion, saltines, mint, 3 tablespoons gochujang, egg, and ½ teaspoon salt. Mold meat mixture into a large loaf on baking sheet.

2   In a medium bowl, whisk oil with 4 tablespoons gochujang, coriander, and 1 teaspoon salt. Add green beans and toss to coat. On a separate rimmed baking sheet, evenly distribute green beans.

3   Roast meatloaf and green beans in the oven for 25 minutes. While roasting, toss green beans twice.

4   While the meatloaf and green beans are in the oven, combine ketchup and 2 tablespoons gochujang in a small bowl. After 25 minutes, remove the meatloaf from the oven and brush the ketchup mixture over the meatloaf. Return meatloaf to oven and bake for an additional 30 minutes, or until cooked through (160°F).

EACH SERVING: ABOUT 395 CALORIES, 25G PROTEIN, 24G CARBOHYDRATE, 23G TOTAL FAT (7G SATURATED), 5G FIBER, 1,001MG SODIUM.

TIP

While gochujang (pronounced go-choo-jong) makes a killer meatloaf glaze, it also works well doused on grilled meats, stir-fries, and roasted veggies.

Feta & Mint
MINI MEATLOAVES

This American classic takes a Mediterranean spin
with the addition of feta, mint, and green olives.

ACTIVE TIME: 10 MINUTES **TOTAL TIME:** 30 MINUTES
MAKES: 4 SERVINGS

1¼ **pounds ground beef chuck**

½ **cup crumbled feta cheese**

½ **cup fresh mint, finely chopped**

Salt

1 **large leek, sliced**

3 **medium yellow squash, chopped**

1 **cup pitted green olives**

1 **tablespoon olive oil**

1 Preheat oven to 450°F. In a large bowl,
combine ground beef chuck, feta cheese, mint,
and ¼ teaspoon salt. Form meat mixture into
4 mini loaves and place them on a foil-lined
baking sheet.

2 In another bowl, toss leek, yellow squash, and
green olives, oil, and ⅛ teaspoon salt. Arrange
the vegetables around mini loaves on baking
sheet. Roast in the oven for 15 to 20 minutes, or
until meatloaves are cooked through (165°F).

EACH SERVING: ABOUT 415 CALORIES, 30G PROTEIN,
12G CARBOHYDRATE, 28G TOTAL FAT (10G SATURATED),
4G FIBER, 935MG SODIUM.

Cheeseburger
TOSTADAS

Craft pickles are the perfect topping for this
American-Mexican fusion meal.

ACTIVE TIME: 10 MINUTES **TOTAL TIME:** 22 MINUTES
MAKES: 4 SERVINGS

4   medium flour tortillas

8   ounces ground beef, cooked

1   cup shredded Cheddar cheese

Salt

Shredded lettuce

Chopped tomatoes

Dill pickles, chopped

Ketchup, for serving

1 Preheat oven to 475°F. Coat two baking sheets
with nonstick cooking spray. Place 2 tortillas on
each baking sheet. Top each tortilla with beef
and cheese. Distribute ¼ teaspoon salt across
all tortillas. Bake in the oven for 12 minutes.

2 After removing the baking sheets from the
oven, top each tortilla with lettuce, tomatoes,
and dill pickles. Drizzle each tortilla with
ketchup, if desired.

EACH SERVING: ABOUT 375 CALORIES, 22G PROTEIN,
29G CARBOHYDRATE, 19G TOTAL FAT (9G SATURATED),
2G FIBER, 880MG SODIUM.

Greek-Style
MEATBALLS

These delicious meatballs are served with roasted potato wedges
and a refreshing cucumber-yogurt sauce.

ACTIVE TIME: 10 MINUTES   **TOTAL TIME:** 30 MINUTES
MAKES: 4 SERVINGS

1   pound ground beef

¾   cup feta cheese, crumbled

½   small red onion

⅓   cup Italian-style bread crumbs

¼   cup fresh parsley, chopped

1   large egg

2   teaspoons dried oregano

Salt

Freshly ground black pepper

1   pound red potatoes, cut into wedges

2   teaspoons olive oil

Lemon slices

½   cup prepared tzatziki

Parsley, for garnish

1 Preheat the oven to 425°F. In large bowl, mix
ground beef, feta cheese, red onion, bread crumbs,
fresh parsley, egg, dried oregano, ¼ teaspoon each
salt and pepper. Form meat mixture into 12 balls
and thread 3 onto each skewer.

2 In another bowl, toss potatoes with 2 teaspoons
oil. Spread potatoes in single layer on a baking
sheet. Season to taste before placing in the oven
to roast.

3 Coat another baking sheet with nonstick
cooking spray. Arrange skewers on baking sheet.
Roast the meatballs in the oven for 15 to 20
minutes, or until cooked through. Remove the
meatballs from the oven, but allow the potatoes to
roast for an additional 15 minutes or until crispy
yet tender.

3 Serve meatballs with lemon slices, tzatziki, and
potatoes. Garnish with additional parsley.

....

EACH SERVING: ABOUT 480 CALORIES, 33G PROTEIN,
31G CARBOHYDRATE, 25G TOTAL FAT (11G SATURATED),
2G FIBER, 990MG SODIUM.

TIP

Before preparing kebabs, soak skewers in
water for 30 minutes to prevent the wood
from charring while in the oven.

Meatball-Mozzarella
PIZZA

Prepare extra meatballs to bake and another dinner will be prepared when needed. For photo, see page 44.

ACTIVE TIME: 15 MINUTES   **TOTAL TIME:** 40 MINUTES
MAKES: 6 SERVINGS

1¼-pounds ball of pizza dough or Easy Homemade Dough (page 15)

1   cup shredded mozzarella

2   plum tomatoes, thinly sliced

½   small red onion, thinly sliced

Freshly ground black pepper

8   ounces ground beef chuck or ground turkey

¼   cup seasoned (Italian) bread crumbs

Salt

1   Preheat oven to 450°F. Place a large baking sheet in oven. On a large sheet of parchment, stretch and roll pizza dough to a 13-inch circle. Top the dough with mozzarella, tomatoes, red onion, and ¼ teaspoon pepper.

2   In a large bowl, combine beef or turkey, bread crumbs, and a pinch of salt. Form meat mixture into 1-inch meatballs and place meatballs on the pizza. Spray pizza with nonstick cooking spray. Remove baking sheet from the oven. Carefully slide pizza from parchment paper onto preheated baking sheet. Bake 20 to 25 minutes, or until bottom of crust is golden brown.

EACH SERVING: ABOUT 395 CALORIES, 18G PROTEIN, 48G CARBOHYDRATE, 13G TOTAL FAT (5G SATURATED), 2G FIBER, 1,130MG SODIUM.

TIP

Be gentle when shaping meatballs. Tightly packed meatballs will dry out during cooking.

Stuffed Tomatoes
WITH LEAN GROUND BEEF

A stellar source of iron and vitamin C, this Mediterranean dish features a savory combination of feta, mint, and brown rice.

ACTIVE TIME: 30 MINUTES **TOTAL TIME:** 1 HOUR
MAKES: 6 SERVINGS

½ cup brown rice

1 tablespoon olive oil

1 medium onion

1¼ pounds ground beef

⅓ cup mint leaves, chopped

½ teaspoon ground cinnamon

Salt

Freshly ground black pepper

6 large tomatoes

½ cup feta cheese

¼ cup panko bread crumbs

Mint sprigs, for garnish

1 Preheat oven to 425°F. In 3-quart saucepan, cook rice according to package instructions.

2 Meanwhile, in 12-inch nonstick skillet, heat oil on medium for 1 minute. Add onion, and cook 10 to 12 minutes, or until lightly browned and tender. Stir in ground beef, half of mint, cinnamon, ¼ teaspoon each salt and pepper. Cook 5 to 6 minutes, or until beef browns, breaking up meat with spatula and stirring occasionally. Stir in remaining mint.

3 While ground beef cooks, cut each tomato in half horizontally. With melon baller or spoon, scoop out tomato pulp and place it in a large bowl. Remove 1 cup tomato pulp from bowl and chop. Discard remaining pulp. Return chopped pulp to bowl. Add rice, feta cheese, and beef mixture; stir until well blended.

4 In 15½ x 10½-inch jelly-roll pan, place tomato halves, cut sides up. Mound scant ½ cup beef filling in each tomato half. Sprinkle the tops with panko. Bake tomatoes for 25 to 30 minutes, or until crumbs are browned and filling is heated through. Garnish with mint sprigs and serve.

....

EACH SERVING: ABOUT 270 CALORIES, 26G PROTEIN, 21G CARBOHYDRATE, 10G TOTAL FAT (3G SATURATED), 4G FIBER, 285MG SODIUM.

Roast Beef
WITH HORSERADISH CREAM

A juicy seasoned sirloin roast is the centerpiece of this delicious dish. With a side of roasted potatoes, it's sure to be a family favorite.

ACTIVE TIME: 15 MINUTES   **TOTAL TIME:** 45 MINUTES
MAKES: 6 SERVINGS

4   cloves garlic

2   sprigs fresh rosemary

Olive oil

Salt

Freshly ground black pepper

1½ pounds Yukon Gold potatoes

1   whole tri-tip (sirloin tip) roast

¼   cup heavy or whipping cream

2   tablespoons prepared horseradish

½   teaspoon Dijon mustard

½   teaspoon white wine vinegar

1 Preheat oven to 475°F. With side of knife, gently smash 3 cloves garlic; discard peel. Into small bowl, crush remaining clove garlic with press. Cut 1 rosemary sprig into 1-inch pieces; set aside. Remove leaves from other sprig; discard stem. Finely chop leaves and add to bowl with crushed garlic along with 1 teaspoon oil, ¼ teaspoon each salt and pepper; set aside.

2 In 18 x 12-inch jelly-roll pan, combine potatoes, 1 tablespoon oil, smashed garlic, snipped rosemary, ¼ teaspoon each salt and pepper until well mixed. Spread in even layer, making space in center of pan for beef. Place beef in center of pan, fat side down; rub with reserved garlic-rosemary mixture.

3 Roast in the oven for 20 minutes or until beef browns. Reset oven to 350°F and continue to roast for 8 to 10 minutes, or until temperature on meat thermometer, inserted into thickest part of beef, reaches 130°F; transfer to cutting board. Cover loosely and let meat stand for 10 minutes. Transfer potatoes to platter.

4 Meanwhile, whisk cream, horseradish, mustard, vinegar, ⅛ teaspoon each salt and pepper until well blended. Slice meat thinly; serve with potatoes and horseradish cream.

EACH SERVING: ABOUT 360 CALORIES, 32G PROTEIN, 16G CARBOHYDRATE, 19G TOTAL FAT (7G SATURATED), 2G FIBER, 335MG SODIUM.

TIP

When roasting a large cut of meat, allow to stand at room temperature for 1 hour before placing in the oven.

Slow Roasted Lamb
WITH PISTACHIO GREMOLATA

The pistachio topping adds great texture to this delightful and succulent dinner.

ACTIVE TIME: 20 MINUTES   **TOTAL TIME:** 1 HOUR 45 MINUTES
MAKES: 6 SERVINGS

3   cloves garlic, finely chopped

2   teaspoons ground coriander

Salt

Freshly ground black pepper

1   boneless leg of lamb (about 4 pounds), trimmed of excess fat

1   pound thin carrots, quartered lengthwise

1   pound parsnips, quartered lengthwise

2   medium leeks, sliced

2   tablespoons olive oil

½   cup salted roasted pistachios, shelled

½   cup packed fresh mint leaves

½   cup packed fresh parsley

2   teaspoons lemon zest

1 Preheat oven to 325°F. In small bowl, combine garlic, coriander, 2 teaspoons salt, and 1 teaspoon black pepper. Rub the spice mixture all over the lamb. Roll the lamb into a cylinder. With butcher's twine, tie the lamb in 2-inch intervals to hold its shape. Place the lamb on a rack fitted into a foil-lined rimmed baking sheet. Roast the lamb for 1 hour.

2 After 1 hour, increase the oven temperature to 475°F. Then, in a large bowl, toss carrots, parsnips, and leeks with oil and ¼ teaspoon salt. Arrange the vegetables on another large rimmed baking sheet. Roast vegetables and lamb for 30 minutes, or until vegetables are tender, stirring the vegetables once. The lamb should be cooked to desired doneness or 145°F for medium heat.

3 Meanwhile, on a cutting board, combine pistachios, mint, parsley, and lemon zest and chop finely. Slice the lamb and serve with vegetables; sprinkle with gremolata on top.

EACH SERVING: ABOUT 380 CALORIES, 37G PROTEIN, 22G CARBOHYDRATE, 16G TOTAL FAT (5G SATURATED), 6G FIBER, 715MG SODIUM.

Lamb Sausage
WITH BRUSSELS SPROUTS & CONFETTI COUSCOUS

Sausage is the secret weapon in this super flavorful dish for dinner on the table, effortlessly.

ACTIVE TIME: 5 MINUTES   **TOTAL TIME:** 20 MINUTES
MAKES: 4 SERVINGS

1¼ pounds Brussels sprouts, trimmed and halved

2   tablespoons olive oil

Salt

Freshly ground black pepper

1   pound lamb or pork sausage links

1   cup couscous, cooked

2   medium carrots, finely chopped

2   small sweet peppers, finely chopped

½   cup fresh mint, chopped

1   Preheat oven to 475°F. On rimmed baking sheet, toss Brussels sprouts with 1 tablespoon oil and ¼ teaspoon each salt and pepper. Roast vegetables in the oven for 15 to 20 minutes, or until browned and tender.

2   Meanwhile, line another baking sheet with foil. Arrange sausage links on baking sheet and add to the oven with the Brussel sprouts. Roast for 15 to 20 minutes, or until sausage links are browned and cooked through (165°F).

3   While sausages roast, toss the couscous with carrots, sweet peppers, mint, 1 tablespoon oil and, ¼ teaspoon salt.

4   Serve sausages over couscous with Brussels sprouts.

....

EACH SERVING: ABOUT 340 CALORIES, 25G PROTEIN, 51G CARBOHYDRATE, 36G TOTAL FAT (13G SATURATED), 9G FIBER, 795MG SODIUM.

TIP

If leaves fall off when trimming and halving the Brussel sprouts, do not toss them away— they are still good to roast and will become extra crispy.

Chorizo-Stuffed
ACORN SQUASH

Like an autumn version of stuffed zucchini,
this acorn squash recipe is hearty and filling.

ACTIVE TIME: 15 MINUTES **TOTAL TIME:** 35 MINUTES
MAKES: 4 SERVINGS

2   medium acorn squash, halved and seeded

2   teaspoons olive oil

1½ cups quinoa, cooked

1   cup Manchego cheese

4   ounces dried chorizo, finely chopped

¼   cup mild pickled peppers, drained
    and finely chopped

1 Preheat oven at 425°F. Brush cut sides of acorn squash with oil. On large rimmed baking sheet, bake squash, cut side down, for 20 minutes.

2 In a medium bowl, combine quinoa, Manchego, dried chorizo, and pickled peppers.
After 20 minutes, remove squash from oven. Turn squash halves over on baking sheet. Divide quinoa filling between 4 acorn squash halves. Return baking sheet to oven and bake for 15 minutes, or until squash is tender.

EACH SERVING: ABOUT 430 CALORIES, 18G PROTEIN, 39G CARBOHYDRATE, 24G TOTAL FAT (11G SATURATED), 5G FIBER, 680MG SODIUM.

TIP

Have some leftover chorizo? Stir-fry it with cooked rice, onions, and peas for an easy next-day meal.

Sausage
CALZONES

Hot and golden from the oven, this express-lane meal utilizes prepared ingredients like refrigerated pizza dough and bottled marinara sauce.

ACTIVE TIME: 5 MINUTES   **TOTAL TIME:** 30 MINUTES
MAKES: 4 SERVINGS

1   cup part-skim ricotta cheese

1   link Italian chicken sausage, cooked and chopped

3/4 cup frozen peas

1/2 cup shredded part-skim mozzarella cheese

1   tube refrigerated pizza dough

1   cup marinara sauce

1   Preheat oven to 400°F. In medium bowl, stir together ricotta, sausage, frozen peas, and mozzarella.

2   Coat baking sheet with nonstick cooking spray. Unroll pizza dough on center of baking sheet. With fingertips, press dough into 14 x 10-inch rectangle. Cut dough in half lengthwise and then cut each piece in half crosswise. This will make four 7 x 5-inch rectangles.

3   Place one-fourth ricotta filling on half of one dough rectangle. Fold other half of dough over filling and pinch edges together to seal. Repeat with remaining filling and dough.

4   Bake calzones 25 minutes, or until well browned on top. Serve with marinara sauce.

EACH SERVING: ABOUT 485 CALORIES, 25G PROTEIN, 59G CARBOHYDRATE, 16G TOTAL FAT (7G SATURATED), 4G FIBER, 1,210MG SODIUM.

TIP

Clean out the fridge at the end of the week by making leftover calzones. Mix up this traditional recipe with leftover vegetables and meat instead of ricotta, spinach, and sausage.

Rye-Crusted Pork Chops &
APPLE SLAW

Use leftover rye bread to create an incredibly flavorful coating
for these tasty pork chops.

ACTIVE TIME: 10 MINUTES   **TOTAL TIME:** 25 MINUTES
MAKES: 6 SERVINGS

1   tablespoon olive oil

3   slices rye bread

6   bone-in pork chops

Salt

Freshly ground black pepper

6   teaspoons Dijon mustard

2   tablespoons butter

½   head red cabbage

1   Granny Smith apple

¼   cup red wine vinegar

1 Preheat oven to 425°F. In a food processor, pulse oil and torn rye bread into fine crumbs.

2 Season pork chops with ½ teaspoon each salt and pepper. Arrange the pork chops on an oiled rimmed baking sheet. Top each pork chop with 1 teaspoon Dijon and then press rye crumbs on top. Roast in the oven for 14 to 16 minutes, or until cooked through (145°F).

3 Meanwhile, in large skillet, heat butter on medium-high. When butter has melted, add red cabbage, apple, ¼ cup water, red wine vinegar, and ¼ teaspoon salt to the pan. Heat the cabbage mixture until simmering. Then cover and cook for 10 minutes, or until wilted and soft.

EACH SERVING: ABOUT 355 CALORIES, 26G PROTEIN, 16G CARBOHYDRATE, 20G TOTAL FAT (8G SATURATED), 3G FIBER, 605MG SODIUM.

Roast Pork
WITH WINTER VEGGIES

No need to peel the sweet potatoes for this recipe—just scrub!

ACTIVE TIME: 10 MINUTES **TOTAL TIME:** 30 MINUTES
MAKES: 4 SERVINGS

1¼ **pounds pork tenderloin**

2 **tablespoons tomato paste**

2 **tablespoons fennel seeds**

Salt

Freshly ground black pepper

3 **medium sweet potatoes**

2 **tablespoons vegetable oil**

1 **tablespoon olive oil**

2 **clove garlic**

2 **bunches Swiss chard**

1 **(14-ounce) can no-salt-added white beans**

1 Preheat oven to 450°F. Place pork tenderloin on a large rimmed baking sheet. Brush tomato paste on pork tenderloin and season with fennel seeds, ½ teaspoon salt, and 2 teaspoons pepper.

2 Toss sweet potatoes with vegetable oil; add to baking sheet. Roast pork tenderloin and potatoes in the oven for 25 minutes, or until pork is cooked through (145°F).

3 Meanwhile, in 5-quart saucepot, heat oil on medium. Add garlic and cook 1 minute, constantly stirring. When garlic is fragrant, add Swiss chard and ⅛ teaspoon salt. Continue to stir while cooking for 7 minutes, or until crisp-tender. Then add no-salt-added white beans. Serve Swiss chard with pork and potatoes.

EACH SERVING: ABOUT 450 CALORIES, 37G PROTEIN, 41G CARBOHYDRATE, 16G TOTAL FAT (2G SATURATED), 11G FIBER, 865MG SODIUM.

TIP

Swiss chard is a nutritional powerhouse. It is an excellent source of vitamins, minerals, and dietary fiber.

Roast Pork & Sweet Potatoes
WITH SPICY CABBAGE

This down-home pork tenderloin dinner is a simple dinner solution for a busy weeknight.

ACTIVE TIME: 10 MINUTES   **TOTAL TIME:** 55 MINUTES
MAKES: 4 SERVINGS

2½ pounds sweet potatoes cut into ½-inch chunks

Olive oil

Salt

1¼ pounds pork tenderloin

Freshly ground black pepper

¼ cup barbecue sauce

½ medium head red cabbage, thinly sliced

4 green onions, thinly sliced

1 jalapeño, thinly sliced

¼ cup cider vinegar

1 Preheat oven to 450°F. On baking sheet, toss sweet potatoes with 1 tablespoon oil and ¼ teaspoon salt; roast in the oven for 30 minutes.

2 In a 12-inch skillet, heat 1 tablespoon oil on medium-high. Season pork tenderloin with ¼ teaspoon each salt and pepper. Brown pork on all sides; transfer to baking sheet with potatoes. Brush pork with barbecue sauce. Roast in the oven for 16 minutes, or until cooked through (145°F).

3 To same skillet on medium, add red cabbage, green onions, jalapeño, and ½ teaspoon salt. Cook 12 minutes, or until cabbage is tender, stirring. Stir in cider vinegar.

4 Serve pork with potatoes and cabbage.

EACH SERVING: ABOUT 450 CALORIES, 34G PROTEIN, 52G CARBOHYDRATE, 12G TOTAL FAT (3G SATURATED), 10G FIBER, 910MG SODIUM.

TIP

Want to know what to do with the extra cabbage? Pickle it! Heat 1½ cups distilled white vinegar with 1 cup water, 3 tablespoons sugar, and 2 tablespoons salt. Pour it over shredded cabbage and refrigerate for a day. It'll keep for two weeks.

Pork Tenderloin
WITH MELON SALSA

Melon and citrus tossed in chili powder add fruity
and spicy flavors to an earthy cut of meat.

ACTIVE TIME: 10 MINUTES   **TOTAL TIME:** 25 MINUTES
MAKES: 4 SERVINGS

1¼ pounds pork tenderloin

1   tablespoon olive oil

Salt

2   cups finely chopped cantaloupe

¼   cup fresh cilantro, finely chopped

¼   cup orange segments

2   tablespoons lime juice

½   teaspoon chili powder

Mixed greens, for serving

1 Preheat oven to 450°F. On a baking sheet,
brush pork tenderloin with olive oil; season with
¼ teaspoon salt. Roast for 30 minutes, or until
cooked through (145°F).

2 Combine cantaloupe, cilantro, orange segments,
lime juice, chili powder, and ¼ teaspoon salt.

3 Slice pork and serve over mixed greens topped
with melon salsa.

EACH SERVING: ABOUT 220 CALORIES, 28G PROTEIN,
10G CARBOHYDRATE, 7G TOTAL FAT (2G SATURATED),
1G FIBER, 410MG SODIUM.

Pork Tenderloin
WITH ROASTED-LEMON ORZO

This pork dinner pairs well with a
glass of Chardonnay.

ACTIVE TIME: 10 MINUTES **TOTAL TIME:** 30 MINUTES
MAKES: 6 SERVINGS

2   lemons, halved and thinly sliced

2   pounds pork tenderloin

Olive oil

Salt

Freshly ground black pepper

2   cloves garlic, chopped

2   bunches Swiss chard, chopped

1   pound orzo, cooked

1 Preheat oven to 450°F. Line a baking sheet with parchment paper. Toss lemons and pork with 2 teaspoons oil. Arrange pork tenderloin on baking sheet with lemons. Sprinkle pork with ½ teaspoon each salt and pepper. Roast in the oven for 30 minutes, or until cooked through (145°F).

2 In large saucepot, heat 2 teaspoons oil on medium; cook garlic for 2 minutes. When garlic is fragrant, add Swiss chard. Cover the pot and cook 7 minutes, or until tender. Toss chard with orzo and roasted lemon slices. Serve the orzo with the pork.

EACH SERVING: ABOUT 510 CALORIES, 41G PROTEIN, 63G CARBOHYDRATE, 11G TOTAL FAT (2G SATURATED), 5G FIBER, 505MG SODIUM.

Almond-Crusted Creole Salmon
(page 77)

3 Seafood

Fish can be a finicky protein for many home cooks to get right. Enter your sheet pan. Baking fish fillets—be it a hearty piece of salmon or a delicate white fish like cod—is a healthy and quick cooking method. Change the flavor of the meal with different sauces like Honey-Soy Glazed Salmon with Mushrooms & Peppers or Almond-Crusted Creole Salmon. Add some spice with Roasted Shrimp & Poblano Pepper Salad or Spiced Salmon with Sweet & Tangy Slaw. With minimal preparation and effort, your fish will be tender and perfect.

Honey-Soy Glazed Salmon
WITH MUSHROOMS & PEPPERS

This salmon is presented on a bed of rice with roasted vegetables.
It is a great recipe for easy entertaining.

ACTIVE TIME: 15 MINUTES   **TOTAL TIME:** 35 MINUTES
MAKES: 4 SERVINGS

¼   cup seasoned rice wine vinegar

2   tablespoons toasted sesame oil

⅓   cup light soy sauce

⅓   cup honey

2 to 3   teaspoons chili-garlic sauce

1   tablespoon Chinese or Dijon mustard

1   skin-on salmon fillet

2   packages shiitake mushrooms

1   red bell pepper, sliced

1   large bunch green onions

2   packages instant microwave Jasmine rice

Toasted sesame seeds

Salt, to taste

Freshly ground black pepper, to taste

1 Preheat oven to 475°F. In a medium bowl, combine 3 tablespoons vinegar, 1 tablespoon sesame oil, soy sauce, honey, chili-garlic sauce, and mustard. Set aside ½ cup of sauce in a small bowl.

2 Place salmon, skin side down, on a large parchment-lined rimmed baking sheet. Brush with 2 tablespoons soy mixture.

3 Bake salmon for 8 minutes. In the meantime, toss mushrooms, bell pepper, and green onions with 1 tablespoon of soy mixture.

4 Remove baking sheet from the oven and scatter vegetables around fish. Then brush fish with the remaining soy mixture. Bake 8 to 10 more minutes, or until the fish flakes easily and vegetables are tender.

5 While the fish and vegetables cook, prepare rice according to package directions. Stir rice and remaining 1 tablespoon each of vinegar and sesame oil in a serving bowl; season with salt and pepper to taste. Lift fish from skin with two large spatulas and transfer to a platter with vegetables; sprinkle with sesame seeds. Serve with rice and reserved ½ cup sauce.

EACH SERVING: ABOUT 620 CALORIES, 37G PROTEIN, 83G CARBOHYDRATE, 16G TOTAL FAT (2G SATURATED), 4G FIBER, 1,581MG SODIUM.

Spicy
SOY-GLAZED SALMON

This Asian-inspired dish is low in carbs, high in protein,
and a great way to spice up your week!

ACTIVE TIME: 10 MINUTES   **TOTAL TIME:** 20 MINUTES
MAKES: 4 SERVINGS

5   stalks celery

1   bunch green onions, sliced

4   ounces jalapeños

1   tablespoon olive oil

Salt

4   skinless salmon fillets

2   tablespoons lower-sodium soy sauce

Steamed bok choy

¼   cup unsalted peanuts, chopped

1 Preheat oven to 450°F. On large rimmed
baking sheet, toss celery, green onions, jalapeños,
oil, and ⅛ teaspoon salt. Roast for 15 minutes,
stirring the vegetables twice.

2 On another sheet pan, place salmon fillets
and drizzle with soy sauce. Place the salmon in
the oven with the vegetables for an additional
12 minutes, or until just opaque.

3 Serve salmon with celery mixture and steamed
bok choy. Garnish with chopped peanuts and
remaining sliced green onions.

EACH SERVING: ABOUT 335 CALORIES, 39G PROTEIN,
11G CARBOHYDRATE, 14G TOTAL FAT (3G SATURATED),
4G FIBER, 690MG SODIUM.

Almond-Crusted
CREOLE SALMON

Don't have almonds in the pantry? Use finely chopped pistachios or pecans as a substitution. For photo, see page 72.

ACTIVE TIME: 10 MINUTES   **TOTAL TIME:** 25 MINUTES
MAKES: 4 SERVINGS

1 pound green beans, trimmed

1 tablespoon olive oil

Salt

Freshly ground black pepper

⅓ cup nonfat Greek yogurt

2 teaspoons Creole seasoning

1 teaspoon grated lemon peel

¼ cup almonds, coarsely chopped

4 skinless salmon fillets (6 ounces each)

1 Preheat oven to 450°F. Line large rimmed baking sheet with foil.

2 In large bowl, toss green beans, oil, ¼ teaspoon each salt and pepper. Arrange on sheet pan and bake for 10 minutes.

3 In another bowl, stir together yogurt, Creole seasoning, and grated lemon peel. Spread yogurt mixture onto the salmon fillets and then top each fillet with almonds.

4 Push the beans to one side of pan and place the salmon on other side. Lightly spray the salmon with olive oil cooking spray. Bake for 12 minutes or until salmon flakes easily and beans are tender.

EACH SERVING: ABOUT 310 CALORIES, 39G PROTEIN, 9G CARBOHYDRATE, 13G TOTAL FAT (2G SATURATED), 4G FIBER, 540MG SODIUM.

TIP

Trimming green beans can be done in a snap. Use a chef's knife to cut off the knobby ends with one slice by lining up the stems to face the same direction.

"BBQ" Salmon &
BRUSSELS BAKE

The sugar in this savory rub caramelizes as the salmon roasts.
And leftovers can be tossed with a salad for lunch!

ACTIVE TIME: 15 MINUTES **TOTAL TIME:** 30 MINUTES
MAKES: 6 SERVINGS

2 tablespoons brown sugar

1 teaspoon garlic powder

1 teaspoon onion powder

1 teaspoon smoked paprika

Olive oil

1¼ pounds Brussels sprouts, trimmed and halved

Salt

Freshly ground black pepper

1 fillet of salmon (about 3½ pounds)

Snipped chives, for garnish

1 Preheat oven to 450°F. Line a large rimmed baking sheet with foil. In a small bowl, stir together brown sugar, garlic powder, onion powder, smoked paprika, and 2 tablespoons oil.

2 On another large rimmed baking sheet, toss Brussels sprouts with 1 tablespoon oil and ¼ teaspoon each salt and pepper. Roast sprouts for 5 minutes.

3 Meanwhile, cut salmon into 10 fillets; arrange skin side down on foil-lined baking sheet. Brush rub all over salmon; sprinkle with 1 teaspoon salt. Roast salmon with Brussels sprouts for 15 minutes or until sprouts are tender and salmon is just cooked through, stirring sprouts once halfway through. Reserve 4 smaller fillets salmon for the next day's lunch. Serve remaining salmon with Brussels sprouts. Garnish with chives.

EACH SERVING: ABOUT 280 CALORIES, 35G PROTEIN, 11G CARBOHYDRATE, 11G TOTAL FAT (2G SATURATED), 3G FIBER, 380MG SODIUM.

TIP

The size of a Brussel sprout indicates its flavor—the smaller the sprout the more tender and sweet. Larger sprouts will taste like cabbage.

Spiced Salmon
WITH SWEET & TANGY SLAW

This meal is well balanced with sweetness from the rub on the fish and tang from the vinegar-based cabbage slaw.

ACTIVE TIME: 10 MINUTES   **TOTAL TIME:** 15 MINUTES
MAKES: 4 SERVINGS

1   tablespoon Old Bay seasoning

1   tablespoon brown sugar

Salt

4   skin-on salmon fillets (about 5 ounces each)

½   small head red cabbage, very thinly sliced

½   cup packed fresh cilantro leaves

3   green onions, thinly sliced

¼   cup white balsamic vinegar

1 Turn on the broiler in the oven. Line a rimmed baking sheet with foil.

2 In a small bowl, combine Old Bay, brown sugar, and ½ teaspoon salt. Place the salmon fillets skin side down on the baking sheet. Coat each fillet with the rub.

3 Place baking sheet in the oven and broil on high 5 to 6 minutes, or until the fish flakes easily.

4 While the salmon cooks, toss cabbage, cilantro, green onions, balsamic vinegar, and ¼ teaspoon salt in a medium bowl. Serve the salmon on top of a bed of cabbage slaw.

....

EACH SERVING: ABOUT 305 CALORIES, 30G PROTEIN, 11G CARBOHYDRATE, 16G TOTAL FAT (3G SATURATED), 2G FIBER, 955MG SODIUM.

Fish & Zucchini TACOS

Dry, high heat seals in the succulence and intensifies the smoky flavor of these flaky fish tacos—and makes them a lot healthier than the fried-fillet variety.

ACTIVE TIME: 10 MINUTES   **TOTAL TIME:** 24 MINUTES
MAKES: 4 SERVINGS

2   medium zucchini

1   tablespoon vegetable oil

¼   teaspoon chipotle chili powder

Salt

1   lime

½   cup packed fresh cilantro leaves

1   pound skinless red snapper
    or firm white fish fillets

8   corn tortillas

1   avocado, sliced

½   cup chunky salsa

1 Preheat oven to 400°F. Trim the zucchini and cut each crosswise into 2-inch pieces. Next, cut each piece lengthwise through the centers into 8 wedges. On a baking sheet, combine zucchini, oil, chili powder, and ¼ teaspoon salt and toss to evenly coat the vegetables. Place baking sheet in the oven and roast for 10 minutes.

2 Squeeze 1 tablespoon juice from a lime into a small bowl. Add 2 tablespoons cilantro and ¼ teaspoon of salt to the bowl and stir to combine. Cut remaining lime into wedges and set aside.

3 Remove baking sheet from the oven and push zucchini to one side of pan. Arrange fish in single layer on other side. Sprinkle fish with lime juice mixture. Return baking sheet to the oven and roast for 8 to 10 minutes, or until fish is just opaque throughout.

4 Meanwhile, wrap tortillas in damp paper towels and place in glass or ceramic pie plate. Microwave on high for 1 minute, or until tortillas are warm and pliable.

5 Remove the baking sheet from the oven and break the fish into large chunks. Divide the fish and zucchini among the tortillas. Top each taco with avocado slices and remaining cilantro. Garnish with cilantro sprigs, and serve with lime wedges and salsa.

EACH SERVING: ABOUT 365 CALORIES, 29G PROTEIN, 35G CARBOHYDRATE, 14G TOTAL FAT (2G SATURATED), 8G FIBER, 570MG SODIUM.

Fish & CHIPS

Avoid making a mess and crush the chips for the coating in the bag.
Make a small hole in the top and go to town with a rolling pin.

ACTIVE TIME: 10 MINUTES **TOTAL TIME:** 30 MINUTES
MAKES: 4 SERVINGS

1½ pounds cod fillets, cut into strips

3 large egg whites, beaten

6 ounces salt-and-vinegar potato chips, finely crushed

Salt

1 pound frozen peas

3 tablespoons butter

1 tablespoon lemon juice

Freshly ground black pepper

Lemon wedges, for serving

Chives, for garnish

1 Preheat oven to 450°F. Line a large baking sheet with foil and spray generously with nonstick spray. Dip each cod fillet into egg whites, then into the potato chip coating. Arrange fish fillets on the prepared baking sheet, placing them evenly apart. Spray the fish with nonstick cooking spray.

2 Place in the oven and bake for 12 minutes. Remove the baking sheet from the oven. Sprinkle with ¼ teaspoon salt.

3 Meanwhile, combine the frozen peas, butter, lemon juice, ¼ teaspoon salt, and ½ teaspoon pepper in a medium bowl. Microwave the peas on high for 5 minutes. Pour peas into a food processor and puree until smooth.

4 Remove the baking sheet with fish from the oven. Serve fish with peas and lemon wedges, and garnish with chives.

EACH SERVING: ABOUT 295 CALORIES, 35G PROTEIN, 16G CARBOHYDRATE, 10G TOTAL FAT (6G SATURATED), 6G FIBER, 570MG SODIUM.

TIP

No cod at the market? Use another mild and delicate white fish like flounder or tilapia but always make sure to use fresh fish.

Bass Packet
WITH TOMATO, CORN, CHICKPEAS & OLIVES

Baking the fish en papillote, or in parchment,
ensures it won't dry out in the oven.

ACTIVE TIME: 10 MINUTES **TOTAL TIME:** 25 MINUTES
MAKES: 4 SERVINGS

1   cup fresh corn kernels from 2 ears

1   cup canned chickpeas, rinsed

4   ounces green beans, trimmed

½   pound small tomatoes (about 2),
cut into 8 wedges

⅓   cup pitted green olives, chopped

2   tablespoons extra-virgin olive oil

Salt

Freshly ground black pepper

4   (6-ounce) skinless bass, halibut, or cod fillets

4   sprigs oregano

1 Preheat oven to 425°F. Place corn, chickpeas, green beans, tomatoes, and olives on one side of four 11 x 15-inch pieces of parchment paper, dividing evenly. Drizzle with oil, dividing evenly, and season with salt and pepper.

2 Season fish with salt and pepper and top with oregano; place the one fish fillet in each packet on top of the vegetables.

3 Fold parchment over fish and vegetables, then fold edges under twice to seal. Transfer packets to baking sheet and bake until fish is opaque throughout, 12 to 15 minutes.

4 Carefully tear open packets to serve.

....

EACH SERVING: ABOUT 340 CALORIES, 36G PROTEIN, 20G CARBOHYDRATE, 14G TOTAL FAT (2G SATURATED), 5G FIBER, 507MG SODIUM.

TIP

This cooking technique can also be used on the grill by substituting aluminum foil for parchment paper.

Cod
WITH SPANISH-MUSHROOM RELISH

Meaty, flaky cod is the perfect anchor
for this Spanish-inspired meal.

ACTIVE TIME: 20 MINUTES   **TOTAL TIME:** 20 MINUTES
MAKES: 4 SERVINGS

Olive oil

1   small shallot

1   package sliced mushrooms

1   cup halved grape tomatoes

½   cup chopped green olives

4   ounces cooked chorizo sausage

Salt

1   pound thin green beans

4   skinless cod fillets

1   teaspoon smoked paprika

1   Preheat oven to 450°F. While the oven preheats, add 1 tablespoon oil to a 12-inch skillet over medium heat. When the oil is hot, add shallot and sliced mushrooms. Cook for 5 minutes, while stirring, or until soft. Add grape tomatoes, green olives, chorizo sausage, and ¼ teaspoon salt. Cook 5 additional minutes, or until vegetables soften.

2   Meanwhile, microwave green beans and 2 tablespoons water in covered bowl on high for 3 minutes. When done cooking, drain the water.

3   In the same bowl, toss beans with 1 tablespoon oil. Spread the vegetables on 1 side of a jelly-roll pan. Arrange cod fillets on other side of pan. Season fish with smoked paprika and ½ teaspoon salt. Roast the fish and vegetables in the oven for 8 to 10 minutes, or until the fish becomes opaque. Serve fish with relish on top and the beans on the side.

EACH SERVING: ABOUT 400 CALORIES, 39G PROTEIN, 15G CARBOHYDRATE, 22G TOTAL FAT (6G SATURATED), 6G FIBER, 1,120MG SODIUM.

Roasted Shrimp &
POBLANO PEPPER SALAD

Roasted poblano peppers give this dinner salad an extra kick.

ACTIVE TIME: 10 MINUTES   **TOTAL TIME:** 35 MINUTES
MAKES: 4 SERVINGS

2   medium shallots, sliced

3   poblano peppers, seeded and sliced

1   tablespoon canola oil

2   teaspoons chili powder

1   pound large shelled, deveined shrimp

4   radishes, sliced

3   tablespoons lime juice

Salt

½   (5-ounce) container mixed greens

1   avocado, thinly sliced

1 Preheat oven to 450°F. In a medium bowl, toss shallots and poblano peppers with canola oil and chili powder. Arrange vegetables on baking sheet and roast in oven for 20 minutes.

2 After 20 minutes, remove baking sheet from oven and add shrimp, spacing them evenly. Return baking sheet to oven and roast for 5 minutes. Then remove baking sheet from oven and let food cool slightly.

3 In a large bowl, combine shrimp mixture, radishes, lime juice, ½ teaspoon salt, and mixed greens. Top with avocado. Divide among 4 plates and serve.

EACH SERVING: ABOUT 215 CALORIES, 17G PROTEIN, 9G CARBOHYDRATE, 12G TOTAL FAT (2G SATURATED), 2G FIBER, 940MG SODIUM.

TIP

If you are sensitive to heat, make sure to remove the seeds from the pepper before roasting.

BBQ Chickpea & Cauliflower
Flatbreads with Avocado Mash
(page 94)

4 Vegetarian

These recipes focus on the perfection of roasted vegetables. Sweet, nutty, and tender yet crisp, these vegetarian meals are still as filling as the recipes in previous chapters. Roasted cauliflower (and chickpeas!) shines in BBQ Chickpea & Cauliflower Flatbreads with Avocado Mash. Butternut squash caramelizes in the Roasted Butternut with Pumpkin Seeds & Mole Sauce Bowls. Grape tomatoes become even sweeter with summertime squash for Two-Cheese Roasted Vegetable Fusilli. In these sheet pan meals, vegetables are not pushed to the side of your plate. They are front and center.

Smoky Tater Hash
WITH FRIED EGG

Although this dish makes a great breakfast-for-dinner option,
you can also prepare ahead for delicious morning meals.

ACTIVE TIME: 5 MINUTES   **TOTAL TIME:** 30 MINUTES
MAKES: 4 SERVINGS

1   pound frozen potato puffs

8   ounces mixed mushrooms, thinly sliced

½   cup roasted red peppers, drained
    and chopped

1   medium onion, finely chopped

1½   tablespoons olive oil

½   teaspoon smoked paprika

Salt

Fried egg, for serving

1 Preheat oven to 425°F. In a large bowl, toss potato puffs with mushrooms, red peppers, onion, oil, smoked paprika, and ¼ teaspoon salt. Arrange in single layer on two large rimmed baking sheets.

2 Bake at 425°F for 25 minutes, rotating pans on oven racks halfway through. Serve topped with a fried egg.

EACH SERVING: ABOUT 355 CALORIES, 10G PROTEIN, 34G CARBOHYDRATE, 21G TOTAL FAT (4G SATURATED), 4G FIBER, 760MG SODIUM.

TIP

For perfect sunny-side up eggs, cook over medium heat, covering skillet with a lid to capture steam.

BBQ Chickpea & Cauliflower
FLATBREADS WITH AVOCADO MASH

Move over, avocado toast—this is your new vegetarian go-to meal. Crunchy roasted chickpeas and tender cauliflower amp up this crowd favorite. For photo, see page 90.

ACTIVE TIME: 20 MINUTES   **TOTAL TIME:** 45 MINUTES
MAKES: 4 SERVINGS

½ can (about 1 cup) chickpeas

Extra-virgin olive oil

Salt

Freshly ground black pepper

12 ounces small cauliflower florets

¼ teaspoon dark brown sugar

⅛ teaspoon ground cumin

⅛ teaspoon ground paprika

⅛ teaspoon garlic powder

⅛ teaspoon chili powder

2 ripe avocados

2 tablespoons lemon juice

4 flatbreads or pocketless pitas, toasted

2 tablespoons roasted salted pepitas

Hot sauce, for serving

1 Preheat oven to 425°F. In the meantime, rinse and drain chickpeas in a colander. Pat the chickpeas with a paper towel until very dry, discarding any loose skins.

2 On large rimmed baking sheet, toss chickpeas with ½ tablespoon oil and season with salt and pepper. On a second large rimmed baking sheet, toss cauliflower with 1 tablespoon oil and ¼ teaspoon salt.

3 Place both baking sheets in the oven and roast for 25 minutes. While roasting, shake the baking sheet with chickpeas occasionally.

4 After 25 minutes, remove baking sheets from oven and let cool. Transfer chickpeas to a bowl and toss with brown sugar, cumin, paprika, garlic powder, and chili powder. Chickpeas will continue to crisp as they cool. Set aside.

5 Mash avocado with lemon juice and a pinch of salt. Spread avocado over flatbreads. Top flatbreads with roasted cauliflower, chickpeas, and pepitas. Drizzle each flatbread with hot sauce and serve.

EACH SERVING: ABOUT 500 CALORIES, 11G PROTEIN, 65G CARBOHYDRATE, 25G TOTAL FAT (4G SATURATED), 13G FIBER, 915MG SODIUM.

TIP

Roasted chickpeas make a great low-calorie snack. For a sweeter variation, toss them with 2 tablespoons maple syrup, 2 teaspoons sugar, 1 teaspoon cinnamon, and ¼ teaspoon nutmeg. Return to the oven for 5 minutes until caramelized.

Roasted Butternut Squash
WITH PUMPKIN SEEDS & MOLE SAUCE BOWLS

This vegetarian squash bowl is so hearty and luscious
you'll hardly miss the meat.

ACTIVE TIME: 10 MINUTES   **TOTAL TIME:** 50 MINUTES
MAKES: 4 SERVINGS

1   large butternut squash, peeled and cut into 1-inch chunks

Olive oil

Salt

Freshly ground black pepper

½   cup raw shelled pumpkin seeds, plus more for garnish

½   teaspoon cumin seeds

½   teaspoon dried oregano

½   onion, cut into wedges

2   tomatillos, husked and halved

2   cloves garlic, halved

1   jalapeño, sliced

¾   cup vegetable stock

½   cup coconut milk

½   cup parsley, chopped

¼   cup packed cilantro, chopped, plus more for garnish

Lime wedges, for garnish

Cooked rice, for serving

1   Preheat oven to 400°F. Toss squash with 2 tablespoons oil, 1 teaspoon salt, and ¼ teaspoon pepper. Arrange on baking sheet; roast 35 to 40 minutes, or until squash is tender, stirring occasionally.

2   Meanwhile, in 10-inch skillet, toast pumpkin seeds, cumin seeds, and oregano on medium for 3 minutes, or until fragrant, stirring. Remove from heat; set aside. In same skillet, heat 1 tablespoon oil on medium. Add onion, tomatillos, garlic, and jalapeño; cook 5 minutes or until slightly browned. Place vegetables, pumpkin seeds, and spice mixture in blender or food processor. Pulse a few times; then add stock, coconut milk, parsley, cilantro, ¾ teaspoon salt, and ¼ teaspoon pepper. Process until smooth. Makes 3 cups.

3   Return mixture to skillet; simmer on medium stirring often, 15 to 20 minutes, or until slightly thickened. Divide rice and squash among four bowls; dollop with sauce. Serve remaining sauce on the side. Garnish with cilantro and lime wedges.

EACH SERVING: ABOUT 440 CALORIES, 10G PROTEIN, 60G CARBOHYDRATE, 19G TOTAL FAT (6G SATURATED), 5G FIBER, 605MG SODIUM.

Butternut Squash
TART

This tart is simple to create, looks beautiful,
and utilizes seasonal produce.

ACTIVE TIME: 10 MINUTES   **TOTAL TIME:** 35 MINUTES
MAKES: 4 SERVINGS

1   small butternut squash

8   sheets phyllo dough

1   cup pure pumpkin

½   cup grated Parmesan cheese

Salt

Freshly ground black pepper

2   tablespoons butter

¼   cup torn sage leaves

¼   cup walnuts, chopped

4   cups frisée

2   tablespoons lemon juice

1 Preheat oven to 450°F.

2 Put butternut squash and 2 tablespoons water in bowl; cover. Microwave on high 5 minutes, or until tender; drain.

3 Meanwhile, stack 8 sheets phyllo dough on parchment-lined cookie sheet, spraying olive oil cooking spray between each layer. If you do not have spray olive oil, brush olive oil between the layers using a pastry brush.

4 Mix pumpkin, Parmesan, and ¼ teaspoon each salt and pepper; spread on phyllo, leaving 2-inch border. Top with squash, melted butter, torn sage leaves, and walnuts. Fold edges in. Bake 15 to 20 minutes, or until golden.

5 Serve with frisée tossed with lemon juice and ¼ teaspoon salt.

EACH SERVING: ABOUT 325 CALORIES, 10G PROTEIN, 36G CARBOHYDRATE, 17G TOTAL FAT (6G SATURATED), 6G FIBER, 695MG SODIUM.

Winter Vegetable TART

A delicious dinner, this tart would also make a great appetizer
at your next dinner party.

ACTIVE TIME: 45 MINUTES   **TOTAL TIME:** 1 HOUR 45 MINUTES
MAKES: 10 SERVINGS (2 TARTS)

3   cups all-purpose flour

Salt

1½   cups butter

¾   cup ice water

8   ounces radishes

8   ounces Brussels sprouts

2   medium carrots

2   small red onions

Extra-virgin olive oil

4   cloves garlic

2   bunches Swiss chard

8   ounces Gruyère cheese

1 Preheat oven to 400°F. In food processor, pulse flour and ¾ teaspoon salt until combined. Add half of butter, pulsing until fine crumbs form. Add remaining butter, pulsing just until coarse crumbs form. Drizzle half of ice water over flour mixture, pulsing to incorporate. Drizzle in remaining ice water; pulse until dough mostly comes together. Transfer dough to large bowl; knead 3 or 4 times until dough fully comes together. Divide into two equal-size disks; wrap in plastic. Refrigerate at least 30 minutes or up to 2 days.

2 Meanwhile, in large bowl, toss radishes, Brussels sprouts, carrots, and onions with 2 tablespoons oil and ½ teaspoon salt; arrange in single layer on two large rimmed baking sheets. Roast 25 minutes, or until browned and almost tender, stirring once. Vegetables can be made up to 1 day ahead.

3 In 5-quart saucepot, heat 1 tablespoon oil on medium heat. Add garlic; cook 1 minute, stirring. Add chard. Cook 5 to 8 minutes, or until chard wilts, stems are tender, and chard dries out a bit, stirring occasionally.

4 On large floured sheet of parchment paper, roll 1 disk pastry into 14-inch circle; place parchment with pastry on it onto one large rimmed baking sheet. In center of pastry, arrange half of Gruyère, leaving 2-inch rim on pastry's perimeter. Next, arrange half of chard, then half of vegetable mixture, over cheese. Fold edges of pastry up and over. With remaining pastry disk, cheese and vegetables, repeat rolling, filling and folding process.

5 Bake 50 minutes to 1 hour or until bottoms are golden brown, switching racks halfway through. Remove from oven. Let stand 10 minutes before slicing.

....

EACH SERVING: ABOUT 550 CALORIES, 13G PROTEIN, 36G CARBOHYDRATE, 40G TOTAL FAT (23G SATURATED), 3G FIBER, 815MG SODIUM.

TIP

This recipe prepares two tarts, so if you do not need to serve the second one, prepare for a meal later in the week.

Pizza PRIMAVERA

Crispy and delicious, this pizza highlights
the taste of spring.

ACTIVE TIME: 15 MINUTES   **TOTAL TIME:** 35 MINUTES
MAKES: 4 SERVINGS

1   bunch asparagus, trimmed and
    thinly sliced on an angle

½   small red onion, thinly sliced

2   tablespoons olive oil

Freshly ground black pepper

1   recipe Easy Homemade Dough
    (page 15) or one 1-pound ball
    pizzeria dough

4   ounces Fontina cheese, shredded

1   Place a large cookie sheet in a 475°F oven.

2   In a large bowl, toss asparagus, red onion,
oil, and ½ teaspoon pepper.

3   Stretch and roll out pizza dough into a 12-inch
circle on large sheet of parchment paper. Top
dough with Fontina, then the asparagus mixture.

4   Remove hot cookie sheet from oven. Carefully
slide parchment with dough onto the cookie
sheet. Place in oven; bake 20 to 25 minutes, or
until bottom and edges are deep golden brown.

EACH SERVING: ABOUT 425 CALORIES, 16G PROTEIN,
52G CARBOHYDRATE, 20G TOTAL FAT (6G SATURATED),
3G FIBER, 610MG SODIUM.

Roasted Tomato
& CHIVE PIZZA

No need to slave over the stove for this savory pizza—
just assemble, bake, and eat!

ACTIVE TIME: 10 MINUTES **TOTAL TIME:** 35 MINUTES
MAKES: 4 SERVINGS

1 large pre-baked pizza crust

½ cup olive tapenade

1 cup shredded Gruyère cheese

1¾ cups grape tomatoes

¼ cup mushrooms

Snipped chives

1 Preheat oven to 425°F. Spray a large cookie sheet with nonstick cooking spray. Place pizza crust on pan.

2 Evenly spread olive tapenade onto pizza crust. Top pizza with Gruyère, grape tomatoes, and mushrooms.

3 Spray top of pizza with cooking spray. Bake at 425°F for 20 to 25 minutes, or until bottom is deep golden brown.

5 Remove from oven. Top with chives to serve.

EACH SERVING: ABOUT 355 CALORIES, 17G PROTEIN, 45G CARBOHYDRATE, 14G TOTAL FAT (5G SATURATED), 3G FIBER, 895MG SODIUM.

Bulgur & Cashew
STUFFED EGGPLANT

With no meat or dairy, this heart-healthy meal still has plenty of flavors with the addition of curry and raisins.

ACTIVE TIME: 13 MINUTES   **TOTAL TIME:** 35 MINUTES
MAKES: 4 SERVINGS

Olive oil

3 cloves garlic, crushed

½ cup golden raisins

½ teaspoon curry powder

Salt

1 cup quick-cooking bulgur

2 medium eggplants

½ cup cashews

Chopped mint, for garnish

1 In small saucepot, heat 1 tablespoon oil on medium. Add garlic, golden raisins, curry powder, and ¼ teaspoon salt. Cook 2 minutes, stirring. Add bulgur and 2 cups water. Heat to simmering. Cover; simmer 15 minutes, or until bulgur is tender.

2 Meanwhile, cut eggplants in half lengthwise. Scoop out seeds. Arrange eggplant on foil-lined baking sheet, cut sides up. Brush with 2 tablespoons oil and sprinkle with ½ teaspoon salt. Broil on high (6 inches from heat source) 7 minutes, or until tender.

3 Remove eggplant from oven; cover with foil. With fork, fluff bulgur; stir in cashews. Stuff eggplant with bulgur mixture; garnish with chopped mint.

EACH SERVING: ABOUT 460 CALORIES, 11G PROTEIN, 69G CARBOHYDRATE, 19G TOTAL FAT (3G SATURATED), 16G FIBER, 450MG SODIUM.

TIP

Eggplant has a naturally occurring enzyme that can leave a bitter aftertaste. To ensure it has a sweet and nutty flavor, generously sprinkle kosher salt and let it sit for at least 20 minutes before cooking. The vegetable will sweat; surface liquid can be removed with a paper towel.

VEGETARIAN

Two-Cheese
ROASTED VEGETABLE FUSILLI

Toss together this light pasta dish with summertime vegetables for a quick meal.

ACTIVE TIME: 10 MINUTES   TOTAL TIME: 20 MINUTES
MAKES: 4 SERVINGS

1   pint grape tomatoes, halved

2   large summer squash, chopped

1   small red onion, sliced

3   tablespoons extra-virgin olive oil

Salt

8   ounces whole wheat fusilli, cooked

¼   cup grated Pecorino cheese

½   cup part-skim ricotta

Freshly ground black pepper

Fresh basil

1 Preheat oven to 450°F. In a large bowl, toss together tomatoes, summer squash, red onion, oil, and ½ teaspoon salt. Arrange vegetables on two large rimmed baking sheets. Bake at 450°F for 20 minutes, switching sheets on racks halfway through.

2 Toss vegetables with fusilli and Pecorino. Dollop with ricotta; sprinkle with ¼ teaspoon pepper. Garnish with basil.

EACH SERVING: ABOUT 405 CALORIES, 17G PROTEIN, 53G CARBOHYDRATE, 16G TOTAL FAT (5G SATURATED), 7G FIBER, 420MG SODIUM.

Sweet Potato Cakes
WITH KALE & BEAN SALAD

These sweet potato cakes are balanced with a bright and earthy salad featuring protein-rich black beans and edamame.

ACTIVE TIME: 15 MINUTES   **TOTAL TIME:** 40 MINUTES
MAKES: 4 SERVINGS

3   sweet potatoes, peeled and shredded

2   green onions, thinly sliced

Salt

Freshly ground black pepper

¼   cup light mayonnaise

2   tablespoons lime juice

1   tablespoon soy sauce

5   ounces baby kale

2   (14-ounce) cans no-salt-added black beans, rinsed and drained

2   cups shelled frozen edamame

1   Preheat oven to 450°F. Spray cookie sheet with nonstick cooking spray.

2   In large bowl, toss sweet potatoes, green onions, and ¼ teaspoon each salt and pepper. With ¼ measuring cup, scoop packed sweet potatoes onto pan to form 12 mounds, 2 inches apart. Flatten slightly. Spray tops with cooking spray. Bake 25 minutes, or until browned at edges.

3   In large bowl, whisk mayonnaise, lime juice, and soy sauce. When cakes are cooked, add baby kale, black beans, and edamame to dressing. Toss until coated.

4   Serve cakes over salad.

EACH SERVING: ABOUT 375 CALORIES, 21G PROTEIN, 56G CARBOHYDRATE, 9G TOTAL FAT (1G SATURATED), 16G FIBER, 530MG SODIUM.

Portobello PARMESAN

Stuff mushroom caps with marinara, mozzarella, and bread crumbs for a delicious dinner that will satisfy meat-lovers and vegetarians alike.

ACTIVE TIME: 5 MINUTES **TOTAL TIME:** 30 MINUTES
MAKES: 4 SERVINGS

4 large Portobello mushroom caps

Salt

1 cup marinara sauce

4 slices fresh salted mozzarella

¼ cup panko bread crumbs

Freshly grated Parmesan, for garnish

Sautéed kale, for serving

Sliced baguette, for serving

1 Preheat oven to 450°F. On foil-lined rimmed baking sheet, place Portobello mushroom caps smooth sides down; spray with nonstick cooking spray and sprinkle with ¼ teaspoon salt. Bake in 450°F oven 10 minutes.

2 Spoon ¼ cup marinara sauce into each cap; top each with mozzarella slice, then 1 tablespoon panko. Spray all over with nonstick spray.

3 Bake 15 minutes longer, or until cheese has melted and mushrooms are tender. Garnish with freshly grated Parmesan. Serve with sautéed kale and sliced baguette.

EACH SERVING: ABOUT 395 CALORIES, 22G PROTEIN, 30G CARBOHYDRATE, 24G TOTAL FAT (11G SATURATED), 6G FIBER, 690MG SODIUM.

TIP

Portobello mushrooms are mature cremini mushrooms. To prepare them, remove the stem from the cap. Then, using the tip of the spoon, pry out the black gills. Lastly, cut a series of shallow lines on the cap with a knife to help it soften faster and retain its shape.

Provolone Veggie
PARTY SUB

Score big on game day—this vegetable-packed sandwich
is loaded with goodness, and perfect for a tailgate.

ACTIVE TIME: 15 MINUTES   **TOTAL TIME:** 55 MINUTES
MAKES: 8 SERVINGS

- 1   pound broccoli rabe, trimmed
- 2   medium bell peppers, seeded and cut into eighths
- 1   small onion, thinly sliced
- 2   tablespoons olive oil
- 3 to 4 (10- to 12-inch) hero rolls, split
- 12   ounces marinated artichokes, drained and chopped
- 8   ounces sun-dried tomatoes packed in oil, drained and thinly sliced
- ½   cup pickled pepper slices, drained
- 4   ounces thinly sliced sharp Provolone cheese

1 Heat large covered saucepot of salted water to boiling on high. Preheat oven to 425°F.

2 To boiling water, add broccoli rabe; cook 6 minutes, or until stems are tender. Drain; rinse with cold water. Drain well and gently squeeze dry, then coarsely chop; set aside.

3 On large rimmed baking sheet, toss bell peppers, onion, oil, and ¼ teaspoon each salt and pepper; spread in single layer. Roast 20 minutes, or until brown.

4 Pull some bread from inside bottom halves of rolls; save for another use. Layer bottoms of rolls with artichokes, broccoli rabe, sun-dried tomatoes, onion mixture, pickled peppers, and then Provolone.

5 Arrange on foil-lined cookie sheets. Bake 8 minutes or until cheese has melted; after 3 minutes, add tops of rolls to oven to toast. Replace tops; cut sandwiches into smaller pieces for serving.

EACH SERVING: ABOUT 330 CALORIES, 12G PROTEIN, 33G CARBOHYDRATE, 19G TOTAL FAT (5G SATURATED), 5G FIBER, 720MG SODIUM.

TIP

Use a chef's knife to slice a half inch off the end of the acorn squash. Now with a stable base, halve it lengthwise through the stem. Remove the seeds and then cut into 1-inch slices.

Roasted Winter-Veggie
SALAD

This flavorful dish is the perfect vegetarian meal or
a great side for a festive fall gathering.

ACTIVE TIME: 20 MINUTES   **TOTAL TIME:** 35 MINUTES
MAKES: 4 SERVINGS

1   medium acorn squash

1   medium red pepper

1   medium red onion

½   teaspoon cayenne pepper

Olive oil

Salt

8   ounces small shiitake mushrooms

¼   cup lemon juice

1   tablespoon Dijon mustard

1   large bunch kale

1   (15-ounce) can chickpeas, rinsed
    and drained

½   cup salted almonds

1 Preheat oven to 425°F. Cut acorn squash in
half lengthwise. With spoon, scrape out seeds
and membrane; discard. Thinly slice the squash.
2 In a large bowl, combine squash, red pepper,
onion, cayenne, 2 tablespoons oil, and ¼ teaspoon
salt. Arrange in a single layer on two large
rimmed baking sheets, leaving half of the sheet
empty. Roast 10 minutes, stirring once.
3 Meanwhile, in the same bowl, toss mushrooms
with 2 tablespoons oil. Arrange in a single layer
in empty side of the pan in oven. Roast vegetables
together 15 to 20 minutes, or until mushrooms
are crisp and squash is tender, stirring once.
4 In a very large bowl, whisk lemon juice,
mustard, 1 tablespoon oil, and ¼ teaspoon salt.
Add kale, chickpeas, and almonds, tossing until
well coated. Add all roasted vegetables except
squash to bowl, tossing. To serve, divide salad
between four plates and place squash on top of
the salad.

EACH SERVING: ABOUT 455 CALORIES, 14G PROTEIN,
42G CARBOHYDRATE, 29G TOTAL FAT (3G SATURATED),
12G FIBER, 600MG SODIUM.

Falafel with
CUCUMBER & TOMATO SALAD

Leftovers make a great portable meal. Pack falafel patties and salad into pitas with hummus or tzatziki for a meal on-the-go.

ACTIVE TIME: 25 MINUTES   TOTAL TIME: 45 MINUTES
MAKES: 6 SERVINGS

1   lemon

1   cup fresh mint leaves

3   cloves garlic

1   teaspoon ground cumin

1   teaspoon ground coriander

1   cup packed flat-leaf parsley

Salt

Freshly ground black pepper

2   cans (15 ounces each) chickpeas,
    rinsed and drained

3   tablespoons all-purpose flour

⅓   cup tahini

Extra-virgin olive oil

1   pound tomatoes, chopped

2   seedless (English) cucumbers, chopped

½   small red onion, finely chopped

Toasted pita bread, for serving

1   Preheat oven to 425°F. Spray large cookie sheet with nonstick cooking spray. From lemon, grate 1 teaspoon peel and squeeze 3 tablespoons juice; set aside.

2   To food processor bowl, add mint, garlic, cumin, coriander, lemon peel, ½ cup parsley, and ½ teaspoon each salt and pepper; pulse until finely chopped. Add chickpeas and flour; pulse until just chopped and well mixed, occasionally scraping down side of bowl with spatula.

3   With measuring cup, scoop scant ¼ cup mixture and loosely shape into ½-inch-thick patty; place on prepared cookie sheet. Repeat with remaining chickpea mixture to form 12 patties. Spray tops of patties with nonstick cooking spray. Bake 15 minutes, or until golden brown on bottoms. Turn patties over; bake another 10 to 15 minutes, or until browned on bottoms.

4   Meanwhile, in small bowl, whisk together tahini, 2 tablespoons oil, ½ cup cold water, and ⅛ teaspoon salt until smooth; set aside. In large bowl, toss tomatoes with cucumbers, onion, reserved lemon juice, remaining ½ cup parsley, 2 tablespoons oil, and ½ teaspoon salt. Serve falafel with salad; drizzle with tahini sauce. Serve with toasted pita.

EACH SERVING: ABOUT 436 CALORIES, 16G PROTEIN, 51G CARBOHYDRATE, 20G TOTAL FAT (3G SATURATED), 5G FIBER, 945MG SODIUM.

Sweet & Salty Zucchini Bread Cookies (page 114)

5 Sweet Endings

Cookies and roll cakes are among some of the desserts that are traditionally made on sheet pans. This sweet chapter offers recipes for celebrations and weeknight cravings alike. When using a sheet pan to bake Pumpkin Slab Pie, it will ensure enough servings for a large crowd. Whether made from scratch like the Cannoli Roll Cake or Glazed Berry Tarts or utilizing premade ingredients like ready-to-use pie crust for the Peach Crostata, these desserts are just as easy to make as they are delicious.

Sweet & Salty
ZUCCHINI BREAD COOKIES

Who knew grated veggies could transform into stellar cookies?
For photo, see page 112.

ACTIVE TIME: 5 MINUTES   **TOTAL TIME:** 40 MINUTES
MAKES: 24 SERVINGS

3⅓ cups all-purpose flour

⅓ cup cornstarch

1½ teaspoons baking powder

1¼ teaspoons baking soda

Salt

1¼ cups butter (2½sticks),
room temperature

1½ cups brown sugar

¾ cup sugar

2 large eggs

1 tablespoon vanilla extract

1 cup grated zucchini

¾ cup chopped peanuts

¾ cup broken pretzels

1 Preheat oven to 350°F. In a medium bowl, whisk flour, cornstarch, baking powder, baking soda, and 1½ teaspoons salt.

2 In a large bowl, with mixer on medium speed, beat butter, brown sugar, and sugar until creamy. Beat in eggs, one at a time. Beat in vanilla, followed by flour mixture. Fold in zucchini, chopped peanuts, and pretzels.

3 By scant ⅓-cup scoopfuls, scoop dough onto two large cookie sheets, spacing about 1 inch apart. Bake 20 to 25 minutes, or until bottoms are golden brown. Cool on sheets on wire racks.

....

EACH SERVING: ABOUT 275 CALORIES, 4G PROTEIN, 38G CARBOHYDRATE, 13G TOTAL FAT (7G SATURATED), 1G FIBER, 265MG SODIUM.

Sparkly Apple SLAB PIE

Slabs of apple pie that sparkle with sugar—a must-try, magical fall treat!

ACTIVE TIME: 25 MINUTES   TOTAL TIME: 1 HOUR 30 MINUTES, PLUS CHILLING TIME
MAKES: 12 SERVINGS

3   cups all-purpose flour

1½ tablespoons sugar

Salt

1½ cups very cold butter, cubed

⅓   cup cornstarch

½   teaspoon ground cinnamon

½   teaspoon ground ginger

¼   teaspoon ground allspice

3   pounds Golden Delicious apples,
    peeled and chopped

½   cup brown sugar

4   teaspoons lemon juice

2   tablespoons heavy cream or milk

2   tablespoons coarse sanding
    or turbinado sugar

1 In a food processor, pulse flour, sugar, and 1 teaspoon salt until combined. Add half of the butter; continue to pulse until fine crumbs form. Add remaining butter; pulse just until coarse crumbs form. Add ¾ cup cold water in 2 batches, pulsing between additions and scraping side of bowl. Pulse just until the dough starts to come together. Transfer the dough to a large bowl; gently knead 2 or 3 times until the dough comes together. Divide the dough into 4 equal-size mounds and shape it into flat rectangles. Wrap each piece of dough tightly in plastic. Refrigerate for at least 30 minutes or up to 2 days.

2 When ready to bake, preheat oven to 400°F. Line a 15½ x 10½-inch rimmed baking sheet with parchment paper. Spray the parchment paper lightly with nonstick cooking spray.

3 In large bowl, whisk together cornstarch, cinnamon, ginger, allspice, and ½ teaspoon salt. Add apples, brown sugar, and lemon juice, tossing until the apples are well coated; set aside.

4 Place 1 piece of dough on a lightly floured work surface. Lightly flour the dough. Roll the dough into a 12 x 9-inch rectangle, lightly flouring and scraping as needed to prevent sticking. Transfer the dough to a prepared baking sheet, placing the 9-inch side along the longest side of the pan. Repeat and roll another piece of dough. Transfer to other side of prepared baking sheet, overlapping slightly with first piece of dough. Press seam together to seal. Spread apple mixture over dough in even layer.

5 Repeat the rolling process with a third piece of dough. Place rectangle on top of one side of apple mixture, arranging 9-inch side along longest side of pan. Repeat the rolling process with the remaining piece of dough. Place rectangle on top of other side of apple mixture, overlapping slightly with other piece of dough. Press seam together to seal. Pinch the edges of the dough together to enclose filling. Brush the top with cream and sprinkle with sugar. Cut 4 slits in the top of the crust. Bake for 1 hour and 10 minutes, or until top is deep golden brown. Cool on wire rack before serving. Pie can be made up to 1 day ahead and kept at room temperature, covered.

EACH SERVING: ABOUT 430 CALORIES, 4G PROTEIN, 52G CARBOHYDRATE, 24G TOTAL FAT (15G SATURATED), 2G FIBER, 430MG SODIUM.

Pumpkin SLAB PIE

Roll out our Ultimate Pie Dough on a baking sheet rather than a traditional pie tin so that you can serve this seasonal favorite to a larger crowd.

ACTIVE TIME: 25 MINUTES   **TOTAL TIME:** 1 HOUR 10 MINUTES
MAKES: 12 SERVINGS

PIE

Ultimate Pie Dough

2   cans (15 ounces each) pure pumpkin

1   teaspoon grated peeled fresh ginger

1¼ cups heavy cream

1¼ cups whole milk

4   large eggs

1   cup dark brown sugar

½   cup sugar

2   teaspoons pumpkin pie spice

Salt

Whipped cream, for garnish

ULTIMATE PIE DOUGH

2   cups all-purpose flour

Salt

13 tablespoons butter, cut up and very cold

6–8 tablespoons ice water

1 Preheat oven to 400°F. Place 1 rectangle Ultimate Pie Dough on lightly floured work surface. Lightly flour dough and roll into 12 x 10-inch rectangle, flouring and scraping as needed to prevent sticking. Gently wrap dough around rolling pin and transfer to half of 15½ x 10½-inch rimmed baking sheet, placing 10-inch side of dough along longest side of pan and allowing dough to hang over three sides. Roll remaining piece of dough; place on other half of baking sheet, overlapping slightly with first piece. Press seam together to seal. Trim any excess dough, leaving ½-inch overhang if possible. Crimp and press edges of crust to create even rim, using any trimmed dough to seal cracks or gaps. Cover with parchment paper and pie weights or dried beans. Bake 14 minutes. Remove paper and weights. Bake another 8 to 10 minutes, or until golden.

2 Meanwhile, in 4-quart saucepan, cook pumpkin and ginger on medium-high 10 minutes, stirring often; remove from heat. Let cool slightly. In medium bowl, whisk cream, milk, eggs, brown sugar, sugar, pumpkin pie spice, and 1 teaspoon salt until smooth. Add to pumpkin mixture, whisking until smooth; pour into pre-baked pie crust. Bake 25 to 30 minutes, or until set. Cool completely before cutting. Serve with whipped cream, if desired. Pie can be baked, cooled, and refrigerated, uncovered, up to 1 day ahead.

EACH SERVING: ABOUT 330 CALORIES, 5G PROTEIN, 37G CARBOHYDRATE, 18G TOTAL FAT (11G SATURATED), 3G FIBER, 225MG SODIUM.

ULTIMATE PIE DOUGH

In food processor, pulse flour and ½ teaspoon salt until combined. Add half of butter; pulse until fine crumbs form. Add remaining butter; pulse until coarse crumbs form. Sprinkle 6 tablespoons ice water over mixture; pulse until just incorporated. Pulse in additional ice water 1 tablespoon at a time until dough just holds together when squeezed. Transfer to lightly floured surface; knead gently until dough comes together. Divide into two equal pieces; pat each into flat rectangle. Wrap tightly in plastic; refrigerate at least 30 minutes or up to 1 day.

Cannoli CAKE ROLL

This sweet finale has a rich ricotta and cream cheese filling,
rolled into an orange-liqueur-spiked sponge cake
and topped with whipped-cream frosting!

ACTIVE TIME: 10 MINUTES   **TOTAL TIME:** 1 HOUR 30 MINUTES
MAKES: 14 SERVINGS

CAKE

5   large eggs

1   teaspoon vanilla extract

½   cup sugar, plus 1 tablespoon

¼   teaspoon cream of tartar

Salt

¾   cup cake flour

2   tablespoons orange-flavor liqueur

Confectioners' sugar

RICOTTA FILLING

1¼ cups ricotta cheese

4   ounces reduced-fat cream cheese
(Neufchâtel)

½   cup confectioners' sugar

½   teaspoon vanilla extract

¼   teaspoon ground cinnamon

¼   cup semisweet-chocolate mini pieces

FROSTING

¾   cup heavy or whipping cream

3   tablespoons confectioners' sugar

2   tablespoons orange-flavor liqueur

½   teaspoon vanilla extract

¼   cup pistachios

1   tablespoon semisweet-chocolate mini pieces

1 Prepare cake: Preheat oven to 375°F. Grease 15½ x 10½-inch jelly-roll pan; line with waxed paper; grease paper and dust with flour.

2 In small bowl, with mixer at high speed, beat egg yolks, vanilla, and ¼ cup sugar until very thick and lemon-colored, about 5 minutes. Set beaten yolk mixture aside.

3 In large bowl, with clean beaters and with mixer at high speed, beat egg whites, cream of tartar, and ¼ teaspoon salt until soft peaks form. Beating at high speed, gradually sprinkle in ¼ cup sugar until sugar dissolves and whites stand in stiff peaks.

4 Transfer beaten egg yolks to another large bowl. With rubber spatula or wire whisk, gently fold beaten egg whites into beaten egg yolks, one-third at a time. Sift and fold flour, one-third at a time, into egg mixture.

5 With metal spatula, spread batter evenly in pan. Bake 10 minutes, or until top of cake springs back when lightly touched with finger.

6 Meanwhile, in cup, mix orange liqueur with 1 tablespoon water and remaining 1 tablespoon sugar until sugar dissolves.

7 Sprinkle clean cloth towel with confectioners' sugar. When cake is done, immediately invert hot cake onto towel. Carefully peel off waxed paper and discard. Brush cake with orange-liqueur mixture. Starting from a long side, roll cake with towel jelly-roll fashion. Cool cake roll, seam side down, on wire rack until completely cool, about 1 hour.

8 Prepare ricotta filling: In food processor, with knife blade attached, blend all filling ingredients, except chocolate pieces, until smooth. Transfer filling to bowl; stir in chocolate pieces. Cover and refrigerate filling while cake cools.

9 Assemble cake: Gently unroll cooled cake. With metal spatula, spread filling over cake almost to edges. Starting from same long side, roll cake without towel. Place rolled cake, seam side down, on platter.

10 Prepare frosting: In small bowl, with mixer at medium speed, beat heavy cream and confectioners' sugar until soft peaks form. With rubber spatula, fold in orange liqueur and vanilla. With metal spatula, spread whipped-cream frosting over cake. Refrigerate cake at least 2 hours before serving. Sprinkle top of cake with chopped pistachios and chocolate pieces just before serving.

EACH SERVING: ABOUT 260 CALORIES, 7G PROTEIN, 27G CARBOHYDRATE, 14G TOTAL FAT (7G SATURATED), 1G FIBER, 117MG SODIUM.

Rolling a Jelly-Roll Cake

This technique is surprisingly simple to execute, and the results will look impressive.

Loosen the cake from the sides of the jelly-roll pan. Sprinkle a kitchen towel with confectioners' sugar. Carefully flip the warm cake onto the towel. Started at a short end, gently roll the cake up in the towel. Secure and let it cool.

Once cooled, unroll the cake until it lays flat. Spread the filling of choice on the cake and then preroll the cake to enclose the filling. Transfer the cake to platter with the seam side down. Serve and enjoy.

Glazed Berry TARTS

Pop a handmade raspberry tart in the oven for
a gourmet riff on the toaster favorite.

ACTIVE TIME: 30 MINUTES   **TOTAL TIME:** 45 MINUTES
MAKES: 12 SERVINGS

3 cups all-purpose flour

¼ cup sugar

4 teaspoons baking powder

¾ teaspoon baking soda

Salt

10 tablespoons butter, cut up and cold

¾ cup, plus 2 tablespoons buttermilk

¾ cup raspberry or strawberry jam

1 cup confectioners' sugar

½ teaspoon vanilla extract

1 tablespoons, plus 1 teaspoon milk

Red food coloring and coarse sugar, if desired

1 Preheat oven to 425°F. In food processor, pulse flour, sugar, baking powder, baking soda, and ½ teaspoon salt. Add butter; pulse until mixture resembles coarse crumbs. Transfer to large bowl; stir in buttermilk until dough comes together.

2 Transfer to lightly floured surface; divide dough in half. Roll 1 piece dough into 15 x 10-inch rectangle; cut into six 5-inch squares. Spread 1 tablespoon jam on half of each square; moisten squares' edges with water. Fold pastry over filling; with fork, seal edges. Prick pastry all over. Transfer tarts to large baking sheet. Repeat with remaining dough and jam.

3 Bake tarts 10 to 12 minutes, or until golden. In medium bowl, stir confectioners' sugar, vanilla, milk, and food coloring, if using. When pastries are no longer hot, drizzle glaze over tops and sprinkle with sugar if using.

EACH SERVING: ABOUT 320 CALORIES, 4G PROTEIN, 53G CARBOHYDRATE, 10G TOTAL FAT (6G SATURATED), 1G FIBER, 455MG SODIUM.

Peach CROSTATA

Using a premade pie crust for this crostata makes this summer dessert easy to prepare.

ACTIVE TIME: 20 MINUTES   **TOTAL TIME:** 45 MINUTES
MAKES: 4 SERVINGS

1   **pound peaches, halved, pitted, and sliced ½ inch thick**

3   **tablespoons brown sugar**

1   **tablespoon cornstarch**

⅛   **teaspoon ground ginger**

Salt

1   **refrigerated and ready-to-use pie crust**

1 Preheat oven to 425°F.

2 In large bowl, toss peaches with brown sugar, cornstarch, ground ginger, and a pinch of salt.

3 Unroll pie crust on cookie sheet.

4 Arrange peach mixture on crust, leaving 2-inch border; fold border over filling. Bake 25 to 30 minutes, or until crust is golden.

EACH SERVING: ABOUT 290 CALORIES, 3G PROTEIN, 45G CARBOHYDRATE, 13G TOTAL FAT (6G SATURATED), 2G FIBER, 297MG SODIUM.

TIP

When picking peaches, seek out fruit that are heavy for their size since it's usually a good indicator that the peach is juicy.

Index

Note: Page numbers in *italics* indicate photos on pages separate from recipes.

Photo Credits

Chris Eckert/Studio D: 7

Mike Garten: cover, 2, 10, 12, 19, 21, 25, 32, 38, 44, 51, 59, 63, 72, 78, 89, 90, 112, 117,

iStock: © bedo: 58; © bergamont: 23, 36; © bonchan: 109 (kale); ©chengyuzheng: 42 (scallions), 65; © dionisvero: 49; © duckycards: 62, 122; © Elvaisla: 93; © fcafotodigital: 71; © Floortje: 119 (whipped cream); © ftwitty: 104; © Jamesmcq24: 34 (scallions); © JuliaMilberger: 31; © kaanates: 109 (onion); © lleerogers: 100; © MariuszBlach: 16; © maxsol7: 42; © pjohnson1: 23, 114; © posteriori: 58; © timsa: 76; © Tomboy2290: 80; © tpzijl: 104: © unalozmen: 119 (chocolate chips); © YinYang: 119 (eggs)

© John Kernick: 120

© Ryan Liebe: 75

© Becky Luigart-Stayner: 85

© Johnny Miller: 17

© Danielle Occhiogrosso: 47, 61, 69, 107

© Con Poulos: 56, 97, 99, 111, 123, back cover

Emily Kate Roemer/Studio D: 6, 27, 28, 30, 37, 53, 67, 83, 92, 102

© Kate Sears: 86

Studio D: 7

© Mark Thomas: 119

Metric Conversion Charts

The recipes that appear in this cookbook use the standard U.S. method for measuring liquid and dry or solid ingredients (teaspoons, tablespoons, and cups). The information on this chart is provided to help cooks outside the United States successfully use these recipes. All equivalents are approximate.

METRIC EQUIVALENTS FOR DIFFERENT TYPES OF INGREDIENTS

STANDARD CUP	FINE POWDER (e.g., flour)	GRAIN (e.g., rice)	GRANULAR (e.g., sugar)	LIQUID SOLIDS (e.g., butter)	LIQUID (e.g., milk)
¾	105 g	113 g	143 g	150 g	180 ml
⅔	93 g	100 g	125 g	133 g	160 ml
½	70 g	75 g	95 g	100 g	120 ml
⅓	47 g	50 g	63 g	67 g	80 ml
¼	35 g	38 g	48 g	50 g	60 ml
⅛	18 g	19 g	24 g	25 g	30 ml

USEFUL EQUIVALENTS FOR LIQUID INGREDIENTS BY VOLUME

¼ tsp		=				1 ml
½ tsp		=				2 ml
1 tsp	=					5 ml
3 tsp	=	1 tbsp	=		½ fl oz =	15 ml
		2 tbsp	=	⅛ cup	= 1 fl oz =	30 ml
		4 tbsp	=	¼ cup	= 2 fl oz =	60 ml
		5⅓ tbsp	=	⅓ cup	= 3 fl oz =	80 ml
		8 tbsp	=	½ cup	= 4 fl oz =	120 ml
		10⅔ tbsp	=	⅔ cup	= 5 fl oz =	160 ml
		12 tbsp	=	¾ cup	= 6 fl oz =	180 ml
		16 tbsp	=	1 cup	= 8 fl oz =	240 ml
		1 pt	=	2 cups	= 16 fl oz =	480 ml
		1 qt	=	4 cups	= 32 fl oz =	960 ml
					33 fl oz =	1000 ml = 1 L

USEFUL EQUIVALENTS FOR DRY INGREDIENTS BY WEIGHT

(To convert ounces to grams, multiply the number of ounces by 30.)

1 oz	=	¹⁄₁₆ lb	=	30 g
4 oz	=	¼ lb	=	120 g
8 oz	=	½ lb	=	240 g
12 oz	=	¾ lb	=	360 g
16 oz	=	1 lb	=	480 g

USEFUL EQUIVALENTS FOR COOKING/OVEN TEMPERATURES

	Fahrenheit	Celsius	Gas Mark
Freeze Water	32°F	0°C	
Room Temperature	68°F	20°C	
Boil Water	212°F	100°C	
Bake	325°F	160°C	3
	350°F	180°C	4
	375°F	190°C	5
	400°F	200°C	6
	425°F	220°C	7
	450°F	230°C	8
Broil			Grill

USEFUL EQUIVALENTS LENGTH

(To convert inches to centimeters, multiply the number of inches by 2.5.)

1 in	=				2.5 cm	
6 in	=	½ ft	=		15 cm	
12 in	=	1 ft	=		30 cm	
36 in	=	3 ft	=	1 yd =	90 cm	
40 in	=				100 cm	= 1 m

THE GOOD HOUSEKEEPING
TRIPLE-TEST PROMISE

At *Good Housekeeping*, we want to make sure that every recipe we print works in any oven, with any brand of ingredient, no matter what. That's why, in our test kitchens at the **Good Housekeeping Research Institute**, we go all out: We test each recipe at least three times—and, often, several more times after that.

When a recipe is first developed, one member of our team prepares the dish, and we judge it on these criteria: It must be **delicious**, **family-friendly**, **healthy**, and **easy to make**.

1 The recipe is then tested several more times to fine-tune the flavor and ease of preparation, always by the same team member, using the same equipment.

2 Next, another team member follows the recipe as written, **varying the brands of ingredients** and **kinds of equipment**. Even the types of stoves we use are changed.

3 A third team member repeats the whole process **using yet another set of equipment** and **alternative ingredients**. By the time the recipes appear on these pages, they are guaranteed to work in any kitchen, including yours. **We promise.**